D0955659

Kiss & Tell

Additional illustration and photography credits appear on page 128.

Library of Congress Cataloging in
Publication Number: 2005926115

ISBN: 1-59474-069-0

Printed in China

Typeset in Adobe Caslon, Edwardian Script ITC, Interstate, and
Kepler Ornaments

Designed by Michael Rogalski
Cover Illustration by Kevin Sprouls

Distributed in North America by Chronicle Books
85 Second Street
San Francisco, CA 94105

10 9 8 7 6 5 4 3 2 1

Quirk Books
215 Church Street
Philadelphia, PA 19106
www.quirkbooks.com

A Trivial Study of Smooching

by Kevin Dwyer

Introduction

Remember your first kiss? Of course you do. It's a rite of passage for every living, breathing adolescent. Then again, it really wasn't your *first* kiss; it was just your first real kiss.

After all, is there anyone we don't kiss? Parents, grandparents, spouses, children, friends, neighbors, relatives, relatives of relatives, and strangers all kiss us and receive our kisses, from the day we're born to the day we kiss this world good-bye—and sometimes even after: In many cultures, it's common to kiss a corpse at a funeral.

Kisses are the sweetest element of our cultural tapestry. Sleeping Beauty cheated death with a kiss, Judas ruined everything with a kiss, and Klimt said it all with a kiss. It's a language unto itself, perhaps the most diverse form of nonverbal expression. A kiss says, "I like you," and a kiss says, "We're through." A kiss is innocent here, erotic there.

A kiss gives life, or death. A kiss is a sin. A kiss redeems. *Kiss and Tell* answers every kissing question you've ever wondered about. What makes French kissing French? Why do people kiss the Blarney Stone? Why do people kiss under mistletoe? You'll also discover kissing bugs, kissing fish, kissing cocktails, kissing crusts, and the origins of the phrase "kiss my ass." Along the way, you'll learn about television's first interracial kiss, the first U.S. president to kiss his wife at his inauguration, and the five most romantic movie kisses of all time.

What this book *isn't* is a how-to on the "art of kissing." Kissing can only be learned from real life experience. Practice makes perfect. But reading this book *will* make you smarter, and smart people always make better kissers.

Lip Shtick

What man can turn down a luscious pair of beautiful lips coated in . . . *fish scales?*

That's right. Some 5,000 years ago, long before companies like Chanel and Maybelline came along, lipstick was manufactured using everything and anything—fish scales, ant eggs, even crushed beetles.

Nowadays, this most popular of cosmetics is made using a variety of waxes, oils, pigments, and emollients. Two of the most common ingredients are beeswax and castor oil, but manufacturers have been known to add moisturizers, vitamin E, aloe vera, collagen, even sunscreen.

Yet perhaps the single greatest innovation in lipstick technology came in 1920, courtesy of Preston Sturges—the writer/director/producer responsible for classic screwball comedies like *Sullivan's Travels* and *The Lady Eve*. When Sturges was just sixteen years old, he dropped out of high school to manage a cosmetics company that his mother had started. While there, he invented the first kiss-proof lipstick, ensuring that even after the longest of kisses, those lips stay luscious.

And Only Twenty-Six Calories . . .

It doesn't look like a kiss. It doesn't taste like a kiss. So why is the ubiquitous Hershey's candy named after a kiss?

Because it *sounds* like a kiss. That's the popular opinion within the candy industry, anyway (the company doesn't offer an official explanation). Experts claim that when chocolate is extruded from factory machines, each little dollop makes a kissing sound—*mwtcht!*—as it hits the conveyor belt. The chocolate confections have become so popular, Hershey factories now produce eighty million kisses *every day.*

Tongue Tied

People in the Roaring Twenties kept mixing up kissing with their body parts: Kissing was called necking, and mouths were called kissers. That's what happens when everyone's hopped up on reefer and bathtub gin.

Love Bug

What has six legs, two wings, and the ability to send a person into anaphylactic shock? It's *Triatoma protracta*, a.k.a. the kissing bug, and this is one creature you don't want to make out with.

About one inch long, the kissing bug resembles a cross between a roach and a giant flea. Its preferred habitat is the den of a packrat, an armadillo, or an opossum—but this insect can also thrive in the boxsprings and mattresses of human beings.

Biologists classify it as part of the *Reduviidae* family—a group of critters also known as "assassin bugs." And for good reason. In the dead of night, a kissing bug will creep out of its abode in search of exposed flesh. Since most people sleep under blankets, the bug usually migrates to a victim's face. Once there, it pierces the skin (often the lips, eyelids, or ears) and extracts a nominal amount of blood. The next morning, most victims don't even realize they've been bitten. Except, of course, for the small handful of people who suffer an extreme allergic reaction.

So what's the best way to avoid being "kissed"? Entomologists recommend mosquito netting and frequent housecleaning. We suggest pulling the covers over your head.

Windows to the Soul

Why will many people close their eyes during a passionate kiss? Perhaps because humans depend on sight more than any of their other senses (unlike dogs, for instance, which favor scent). Since our vision is so sophisticated, a large portion of the brain is dedicated to controlling it. But when we "close down" this function by shutting our eyes, we free up brain space to heighten the senses of touch and taste—sort of like deleting a word-processing program on your computer to make room for a game with state-of-the-art graphics.

Bottom line: If your date doesn't close her eyes when you're making out, it's probably a sign she'd rather be home playing *The Sims*.

BIZARRE KISSING LAW #1: Indiana

You can smooch all you want in the Hoosier State—as long as you're clean-shaven. It's illegal for a man with a mustache to "habitually kiss human beings" in Indiana.

"Lord! I wonder what fool it was that first invented kissing."

—Jonathan Swift,
in *Polite Conversation*

Top Ten Kissing Songs of the 1950s

1. "Kiss Me Big" by Tennessee Ernie Ford
2. "Kisses Sweeter Than Wine" by Jimmie Rodgers
3. "'Til I Kissed You" by the Everly Brothers
4. "I Saw Mommy Kissing Santa Claus" by Jimmy Boyd
5. "Kissin' Time" by Bobby Rydell
6. "Who Kissed Me Last Night?" by Rosemary Clooney
7. "Kiss Them for Me" by the McGuire Sisters
8. "A Kiss to Build a Dream On" by Louis Armstrong and Kay Brown
9. "Kissin' Bug Boogie" by Jo Stafford
10. "Kiss of Fire" by Georgia Gibbs

A Wet One for Fido . . . or Not

Doctors recommend against kissing pets if you're allergic to them. Doesn't take a brain surgeon to figure that out, really. But they often also say that children shouldn't be allowed to kiss pets at all in order to minimize the risk of infectious disease. Poor Fido.

These Two Must Have Been Close

According to the *Guinness World Records*, the longest kiss occurred in December 2001, when nineteen-year-old Louisa Almedovar and her twenty-two-year-old boyfriend, Rich Langley, kissed for thirty hours, fifty-nine minutes, and twenty-three seconds. All without eating, sitting down, or even pausing to use the bathroom. They did the marathon lip-lock at *The Ricki Lake Show* television studio for a Valentine's Day special. After finishing up and learning that they'd broken the record, the couple mustered up enough passion for an encore—a quick congratulatory kiss on a job well done.

THOSE PESKY PURITANS

Famous for their bans on drinking, gambling, and Christmas, the New England Puritans were big on self-regulation. And if you weren't able to regulate yourself, they were happy to do the job for you. The first freedom-seekers in America were experts at running their towns with an iron fist, and a smooch on the Sabbath was considered the work of the devil.

A Captain Kemble of Boston, Massachusetts, learned this the hard way. When he returned home in 1656 after three years at sea, the good captain gave his wife a kiss on the doorstep of his home. God forbid! Puritan officials handed down a harsh verdict: For this gross display of "lewd and unseemly behavior," Kemble was put in the stocks for two hours, where he had to keep his kisses to himself.

"ALL THIS—FOR A KISS?!?"

"Last time I was down South, I was in a restaurant and ordered some chicken, and these three cousins—you know the ones I mean, Klu, Kluck, and Klan—they come up and say, 'Boy, we're givin' you fair warnin'. Anything you do to that chicken, we're gonna do to you.' So I put down my knife and fork, and I picked up that chicken. And I kissed it."

—Dick Gregory, comedian

Kissing Hitler

During production of the comedy classic *Some Like It Hot*, Marilyn Monroe drove lead man/woman Tony Curtis nuts by consistently forgetting her lines and mispronouncing words. He vented by telling reporters that kissing Marilyn in the love scene was like "kissing Hitler." Curtis later denied saying it, but his leading lady showed she was above it all. When asked about Curtis's barb, she said that he was just having a hissy fit because she got to wear nicer dresses.

Didn't Hitler have a mustache?

Kissing on the Factory Floor

The next time you *don't* go crazy trying to pry your thumbnail between the corner of a sticker and its backing, you can thank the manufacturing technique known as "kiss cutting." Makers of adhesive decals ranging from Power Puff Girl stickers to DMV registrations will usually print multiple copies of the same image on giant sheets, which are later chopped into individual stickers. Some printers will hack up the sheets like barbarians; others will carefully kiss cut them, slicing around the face material and adhesive without cutting through the nonadhesive backing. It's an incredibly precise process that we don't fully appreciate—at least, not until the corner of that bumper sticker slips and stabs the sensitive fleshy spot beneath the fingernail.

Saved by the Sage

Among his many scrapes with death, Alexander the Great took an arrow in the chest, felt the receiving end of a Persian battle axe, nearly died of thirst in the desert—and came *this close* to being killed by a peasant girl's kiss!

An old Greek tale tells of a country girl who was weaned on deadly poison for the express purpose of assassinating the world's most powerful leader. By the time this human "black widow" reached lovemaking age, her breath was so potent with the poison that anyone she breathed on would die instantly. She was sent to Alexander's palace to seduce the leader and then kill him with a kiss. When the girl arrived, the king immediately fell in love with her—but thankfully his teacher Aristotle was not so easily wooed. Suspicious, the wise old philosopher sent for a criminal and had *him* kiss the temptress. Upon doing so, the criminal dropped dead. Aristotle then called for juice extracted from the dittany root—a magical protection against poisonous creatures. He poured a circle around the girl, which somehow caused her to suffocate. Alexander was saved and went on to raze and plunder more of the world.

All Heated Up

When the heat rises inside an oven, sometimes two loaves of bread will approach each other and kiss. They remain locked together this way until the baker takes them out of the oven and pulls them apart. The spot where they "kissed"—that not-too-soft, not-too-hard, slightly chewy exterior shell—is called the "kissing crust."

"Kiss Me, You Fool!"

We run across this phrase every day and everywhere: in books and poems, on T-shirts and Web sites. Search for the phrase on Google and you'll turn up more than 6,000 hits, enough to make you think it's some kind of famous Hollywood line.

It isn't. The actual dialogue is "Kiss me, my fool," and it wasn't uttered by Marlene Dietrich, Mae West, or any of those other tough broads of the 1930s or 1940s. It came from the toughest broad of all, Theda Bara, who would trounce any femme fatale in a Celebrity Death Match. The first and most ruthless of movie history's "vamps," Bara's real name was Theodosia Goodman. She dressed in clothes that would make Britney Spears blush, applied eyeliner with a paintbrush, and made quite a lucrative career as Hollywood's greatest temptress.

In the 1915 silent movie *A Fool There Was*, Bara plays "The Vampire," a malevolent seductress who exists only to line men up so she can knock them down. In classic silent film–era hyperbole, her intoxicating, feminine wiles would drive men out of their wits. In the film's most memorable scene, one of her victims points a gun at the woman who has ruined his life. Bara, cool as a cucumber, laughs off the threat and says, "Kiss me, my fool." And the man, a fool to the end, turns the gun on himself.

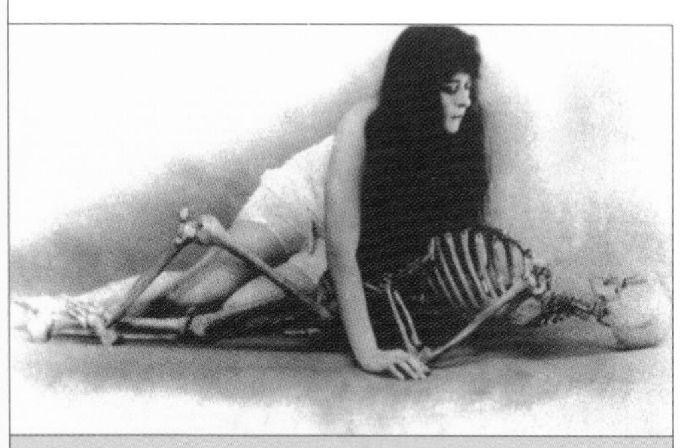
THEDA BARA, FEMME FATALE.

"YOU MAY NOW KISS THE CHIMNEY SWEEP"

Something old, something new, something borrowed, something . . . *filthy*? If you're a bride in England, your husband isn't the only man you kiss on your wedding day. You'll also have to kiss a chimney sweep or (according to legend) the marriage won't last.

Like a lot of traditions, this one has fallen by the wayside in recent years (although some contemporary wedding planners now hire struggling actors to arrive at a ceremony covered in soot). But back in the nineteenth century, the tradition was so prevalent that chimney sweeps would hang around outside churches when weddings were taking place. As the bride left the church, the soot-covered worker would approach and offer a kiss, for which he would often get a tip—a nice supplementary income during the slow summer season.

No one knows how the tradition began. Some cite the legend of a clumsy chimney sweep who slipped on a roof and found himself dangling off the side of a building. A woman engaged to another man reached out the window and saved the chimney sweep's life. The two fell in love and were married.

A 1951 article in the *Journal of American Folklore* offers a more technical origin for the odd custom. Author George L. Phillips cites folklorist Maria Leach, who pointed out that for time immemorial, humans have believed that "both ashes and soot possess magical healing, protective, and fertilizing powers." Members of aboriginal tribes have been known to cover their bodies with ashes in their most sacred rituals. Ancient Jews used ashes in a ceremony to purify the morally unclean, and to this day, Catholics have a cross of ashes applied to their forehead on Ash Wednesday, one of their holiest days. As recently as the last century, even *soap* was made from ashes.

Another reason, according to Phillips, could be that Europeans traditionally began the New Year by cleaning their chimneys (they believed a clean chimney allowed good luck to spread more readily throughout their homes and helped ward off nasty diseases like the Black Death). With such an important responsibility, it's easy to see how the chimney sweep ended up becoming the most popular guy on the block. Both men and women would instinctively blow a kiss to a sweep when they passed one on the street, hoping to ensure an injury-free day.

The Five Most Romantic Movie Kisses of All Time . . .

Gone With the Wind **(1939)**

The kiss shared by Rhett Butler (Clark Gable) and Scarlett O'Hara (Vivien Leigh) is probably the most merchandised kiss in Hollywood history. You can buy framed pictures, music boxes, coffee mugs, snow globes, neckties, and wall clocks of the scene. But no bobble-head dolls. Yet.

To Have and Have Not **(1944)**

Marie "Slim" Browning (Lauren Bacall) sits on the lap of Harry "Steve" Morgan (Humphrey Bogart) and plants a kiss that only a "dame" is capable of. His response—"What'd you do that for?"—is pure Bogie. "I'd been wondering whether I'd like it," Bacall responds, and she kisses him again. Yes, she likes it, indeed.

From Here to Eternity (1953)
It's one of the most iconic kissing moments in movie history—Sgt. Milton Warden (Burt Lancaster) and Karen Holmes (Deborah Kerr) sprawl on a beach while the surf rolls over them—and it almost didn't happen. Apparently, some blockhead suggested the actors try the scene standing up. Good thing no one listened.

Breakfast at Tiffany's (1961)
Animal lovers everywhere cherish this spectacular kiss between Holly Golightly (Audrey Hepburn) and Paul Varjak (George Peppard) because the couple smooches while holding a very disinterested cat. And it's all in the rain, no less.

Lady and the Tramp **(1955)**
Sure, it's a cartoon. But if two adorable dogs smooching over a spaghetti dinner doesn't melt your heart, well, nothing will.

. . . And Five Movie Kisses Just for Guys

Raiders of the Lost Ark **(1981)**
What could be more romantic than a soft kiss on the eyelid when you're heading for Nazi Germany after fighting off Arab swordsmen and poisonous snakes? This tender smooch between Indiana Jones (Harrison Ford) and Marion Ravenwood (Karen Allen) is one of the few times this action extravaganza pauses for a breath. And it's reported to be one of Steven Spielberg's two favorite scenes in the whole movie (the other involves a monkey who salutes Hitler).

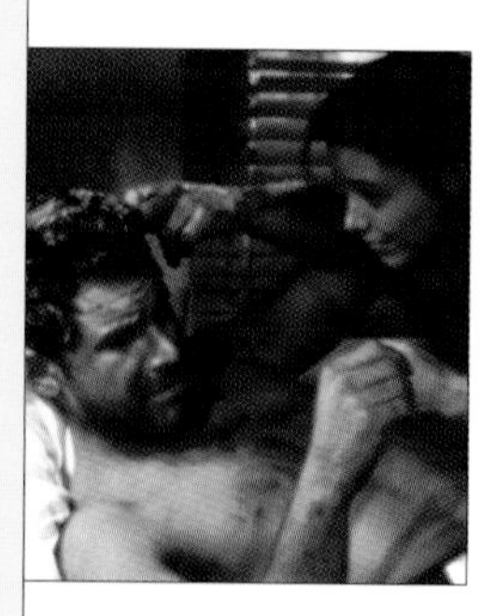

Spider-Man (2002)
While literally hanging on by a thread, Spider-Man (Tobey Maguire) shares an upside-down smooch with Mary Jane (Kirsten Dunst). In an interview with *CNN Entertainment*, Dunst revealed that the mood on the set was anything but romantic: "Tobey couldn't really breathe because [of his] mask. . . . He'd be breathing out of the side of his mouth while we were kissing, so it was really one of the most unromantic kisses, but it looked really romantic and nice."

The Godfather: Part II (1974)
The best "kiss of death" scene there ever was. Michael Corleone (Al Pacino) gives his own brother Fredo (John Cazale) the *Cosa Nostra* kiss of death at a New Year's Eve dance in Havana. "I know it was you, Fredo. You broke my heart. You broke my heart."

A Nightmare on Elm Street **(1984)** "I'm your boyfriend now, Nancy!" Those are the last words heard by Nancy Thompson (Heather Langenkamp) on her parents' telephone before a hideous writhing tongue erupts from the mouthpiece. It's behavior like this that kept Freddy Krueger (Robert Englund) around for seven sequels.

American Pie 2 **(2001)** Two sexy roommates, Amber (Lisa Arturo) and Danielle (Denise Faye), agree to make out in front of Jim Levenstein (Jason Biggs) and Steve Stifler (Seann William Scott)—*provided that the guys do the same for them*. The ensuing hilarity won the 2002 MTV Movie Award for "Best Kiss."

Down and Dirty in the Middle Ages

When you think of kissing in the Middle Ages, you probably picture a knight in shining armor kneeling down and kissing the hand of a blushing maid—unless you've read Geoffrey Chaucer's *The Canterbury Tales*, written around 1390 and now a staple in many high school English classrooms.

In "The Miller's Tale," a local church clerk named Absolon arrives at the window of a carpenter's wife, asking for a kiss. She complies, but not in the way that Absolon was expecting. She sticks her behind out the window,

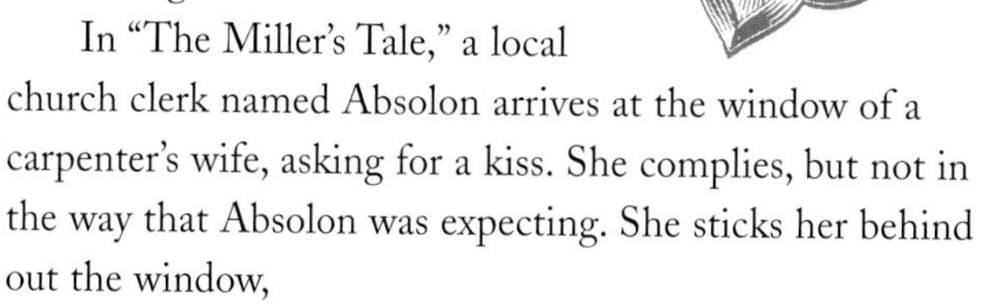

> And Absolon it befell no better or worse,
> But with his mouth he kissed her naked arse,
> Savoring it before he knew what it was.
> Back he jumped and thought it was strange,
> For well he knew a woman has no beard.

With antics like these, there's no telling what Chaucer would have made of *American Pie* or *Animal House*. . . .

SMACK! THE ORIGINAL FROG KISS

PRELUDE TO A KISS.

You've seen it a thousand times: A beautiful princess (often dressed in pink, often wearing a pointy hat) kneels beside a lily pad and puckers up with a slimy green frog. This strange act of interspecies affection dates back to 1812 and a Brothers Grimm fairy tale called "The Frog King." It's the story of a princess who drops her favorite ball into a pond. A frog offers to retrieve the ball on one condition: The princess must agree to be his friend. Unfortunately, this particular princess is a brat. She agrees to the frog's terms, then leaves the amphibian high and dry once she has her toy back.

Later, as she's eating dinner, the frog arrives at her home and tells the king about the girl's promise. The king commands the princess to keep her end of the bargain. The girl grudgingly plays the part of a good friend, sharing her meal with the frog. The frog then announces that he wants to go to sleep, and says he expects the princess to join him. She's horrified by the idea, but the king insists that she take the frog to her bed. As soon as the princess gets to her room, she hurls the frog against the wall—splat! Miraculously, the frog turns into the prince and slides down into the princess's bed. End of story.

Or is it? In 1823, English translator Edgar Taylor decided that British readers wouldn't want to introduce their children to a temperamental princess who ignored her father's commands. So in Taylor's version of the tale, the princess obeys her father's wishes—she tucks the frog into bed and falls asleep beside it. In subsequent versions of the story, the princess adds a friendly kiss good-night. The next morning, she awakens next to a well-rested prince, a reward for her obedience.

"I'd kiss a frog even if there were no promise of a Prince Charming popping out of it! I love frogs. I'd lick him."
—Cameron Diaz, discussing her role as Princess Fiona in *Shrek*

Top Ten Kissing Songs of the 1960s

1. "The Shoop-Shoop Song (It's in His Kiss)" by Betty Everett
2. "Last Kiss" by J. Frank Wilson and the Cavaliers
3. "Kissin' on the Phone" by Paul Anka
4. "Kiss Me Goodbye" by Petula Clark
5. "Then I Kissed Her" by The Beach Boys
6. "Then He Kissed Me" by The Crystals
7. "Hold Me, Kiss Me, Thrill Me" by Mel Carter
8. "Give Him a Great Big Kiss" by The Shangri-Las
9. "Kiss Me Quick" by Elvis Presley
10. "Kiss Away" by Ronnie Dove

If Marriage Is a Prison . . .

Going to Indiana's Vigo County Jail for theft and drug charges was only the start of Jeremy Guinther's problems. In July 2002, Guinther expressed a desire to wed his fiancée, Vivian Frazier, in an in-cell wedding ceremony. Jail officials agreed—but instead of throwing confetti after the bride kissed the groom, they just tacked additional charges on to Guinther's rap sheet.

After the smooch, an observant guard noticed a bulge in Guinther's cheek—and correctly deduced that the prisoner wasn't chawin' tobacco. He ordered the groom to open his mouth, but Guinther took a big gulp instead. The convict soon confessed to swallowing a balloon filled with two grams of methamphetamine. Astonishingly, the blushing bride denied any knowledge of the exchange.

After extracting the balloon "the hard way," doctors confirmed that Guinther's confession was accurate. Frazier received a two-year sentence for trafficking to an inmate. And jail officials created a new rule for incarcerated grooms: You may *not* kiss the bride.

KISSing Across the USA

You can drive from Maine to Florida to California and never lose KISS FM on your radio. Not because there's one single all-powerful KISS FM radio station. Rather, media behemoth Clear Channel Communications has created a gigantic network of radio waves with the KISS moniker all across America. A good amount of what you'll hear is actually recorded at Clear Channel headquarters in California (no matter how convincing your DJ's "local" accent), then dispersed via the company's digital network to the appropriate stations throughout the country.

Animal Magnetism

In early 2004, People for the Ethical Treatment of Animals launched its "Live Make-Out Tour." Animal lovers threw down mattresses on busy sidewalks of such cities as Philadelphia; Washington, D.C.; Boise; Baltimore; and Seattle, then laid down and swapped saliva in front of everyone. The goal: To draw attention to the fact that an all-vegetable diet keeps cholesterol down and the blood (and, by association, other things) flowing at a steady clip, thus making vegetarians better in the sack than those meat-eating brutes. Rumor had it that longtime PETA member Pamela Anderson would be getting back together with her former husband and Mötley Crüe drummer Tommy Lee for an encore performance, but it didn't pan out.

Top Ten Kissing Songs of the 1970s

1. "Kiss and Say Goodbye" by The Manhattans
2. "Kisses of Fire" by ABBA
3. "Great Big Kiss" by New York Dolls
4. "Kissin' Time" by Kiss
5. "One Last Kiss" by J. Geils Band
6. "Kissing My Love" by Bill Withers
7. "Kiss You All Over" by Exile
8. "Kiss an Angel Good Mornin'" by Charley Pride
9. "Kiss in the Dark" by Pink Lady
10. "Merrily Kissed the Quaker" by Planxty

Best Joke About Kissing from *The Simpsons*

Moe the Bartender [*answering his phone*]: Moe's Tavern . . . yeah, just a sec, I'll check . . . [*calling out to the bar*] Amanda Hugginkiss? Hey, I'm looking for Amanda Hugginkiss. Aw, why can't I find Amanda Hugginkiss?

Barney: Maybe your standards are too high.

Klimt's Kiss

If you're a fan of the famous 1907 painting *The Kiss* by Gustav Klimt, you can view the real deal by visiting Austria's Österreichische Galerie. But if that's too much of a trek, don't worry. You can now purchase the painting in the form of shower curtains, cigarette lighters, jigsaw puzzles, handbags, neckties, mouse pads, money clips, candle holders, and business card cases. Die-hard fans can even purchase a pair of *The Kiss* mid-calf boots for $450, or a pair of *The Kiss* golf shoes for $285.

The Kiss (1907) by Gustav Klimt.

XOXO

It's a pretty unromantic way of adding "hugs and kisses" to the end of your letter—so how did XO end up becoming an abbreviation for this phrase?

First of all, get your letters straight. The X is the kiss and the O is the hug. In the days of early Christianity, when most humans didn't know how to write, people would sign important documents, such as land titles, with an "X" instead of a signature. The X pulled double duty, symbolizing Christ's cross, as well as his name (Xristos, in Greek). The signer would then kiss the document as an oath of sincerity.

The O is trickier. No one is sure where it comes from. Some claim that because the circle traditionally symbolizes eternity, it represents some sort of circle of love. Others speculate (rather unconvincingly, we think) that it's a bird's-eye view of encircling arms forming a hug.

BIZARRE KISSING LAW #2: Connecticut

The state is generally tolerant when it comes to kissing, except in the capital, Hartford, where smooching is prohibited on Sundays.

Making Out 101

Has anyone ever said you're a lousy kisser? If you and your partner are in Seattle and have $275 to blow, you can brush up on your skills at a kissing school called (duh) the Kissing School! According to its Web site, the school offers "a safe, playful, and sacred space in which to explore the beginnings of tantra and experience the kiss sublime."

The five-hour kissing class is taught by a psychotherapist in a "safe, nonthreatening environment to gain real education and experiential training in creating a new understanding of intimacy and life through communicating and kissing." Couples are assumed to be heterosexual, but quarterly gay and lesbian classes are also offered. Singles and couples can attend. Couples will practice their kissing only with each other unless they request otherwise; single people switch partners throughout the class. The school also offers this oddly vague warning: "There will be no explicit sex." ("Explicit," huh? Is that a loophole?)

THE KISSING BANDIT

In February 2004, a Branson, Missouri, youth reared his ugly kisser in the wrong place at the wrong time. Nine-year-old Stephen Fogelman—in flagrant disregard for his elementary school's behavior guidelines—chased and kissed a girl on the cheek in his playground. School authorities then chased *him* down and suspended Fogelman for a day.

The school district's handbook states that "sexual harassment" includes physical sexual advances, speech or other expression of sexual desire, and/or creating a sexually hostile situation. The Branson school superintendent ducked out of talking to the press because of ethical concerns about discussing a student's private disciplinary charge. Fogelman's parents, however, were happy to talk to reporters and commented that their son was too young to even know what sexual harassment was. The little girl's parents applauded the disciplinary action, but even they said that labeling the act "sexual harassment" was a tad strange.

"I was babbling on about something, and he just kissed me, kind of to shut me up, I think."

—Monica Lewinsky recounting her relationship with President Clinton, from *The Starr Report*

Glued at the Lips

There's no shortage of sex and nudity in contemporary Hollywood films, but 1941 is still the Year of the Longest Kiss. In the comedy *You're in the Army Now*, Jane Wyman and Regis Toomey kiss for just over three minutes—a feat that earned them a spot in *Guinness World Records* (for "Longest Screen Kiss"). At the time, Wyman was married to future president Ronald Reagan, who reportedly quipped that *he* couldn't hold her attention for that long.

RECORD-BREAKING KISSERS.

Word of Passion

The English language is a hodgepodge of words that hail from many nations and cultures—so English-speakers can't take credit for inventing the word "kiss." Instead, the honor belongs to the same people who gave us lederhosen, liverwurst, and Lutherans: the Germans.

Back in old England—way back, like 1,500 years ago—if you were another poor English-speaker trying to eke out a decent life on some muddy hill, you might ask your beloved for a "coss." The word comes from Old English, the progenitor of modern English, and a language based heavily on Germanic languages. The Old English act of kissing was called "cyssan," and by the Middle Ages, the spelling of the verb had moved toward "kissen" or "kyssen." A stark example of the different noun/verb spellings appears in the Wycliffe Bible of 1384; a line from the Song of Solomon reads, "Kisse he me with the cos of his mowth" (He kisses me with the kiss of his mouth).

The *Oxford English Dictionary* quotes William Shakespeare to demonstrate another trend in the language.

In his 1599 play *Much Ado About Nothing*, he used "kisse" as a noun: "Speake cosin, or . . . stop his mouth with a kisse, and let not him speake neither." The pesky "e" had been dropped by the time Samuel Taylor Coleridge wrote his poem "The Kiss," about two hundred years later: "Ah, why refuse the blameless bliss? / Can danger lurk within a kiss?"

At last we had the word "kiss" that we know and love. As for the origins of the word "smooch," well, that's an entirely different story. Read on . . .

Smooching and Smudging

Some two hundred years ago, a man would receive a "smooch" from brushing against a sooty windowsill, not the lips of his ladyfriend. The *Oxford English Dictionary* traces "smooch" back to the early nineteenth century, when the word meant "smudge." It didn't take on the current meaning of "kiss" until the mid-twentieth century, perhaps after enough men had their cheeks and collars smudged by women's lipstick.

MAKING OUT AT THE MOVIES

Movie history is filled with classic kisses. Clark Gable and Vivien Leigh. Humphrey Bogart and Lauren Bacall. Leonardo DiCaprio and Kate Winslet.

And of course John C. Rice and May Irwin. Maybe the names aren't familiar, but they're the pair responsible for cinema's first swap o' saliva. The Edison Company's film *The Kiss* was a reenactment of a scene from a popular stage show called *The Widow Jones* (the stage actors reprised their roles for the big-screen adaptation). Here's the plot: Rice and his big waxy mustache put the moves on Irwin, who plays a character named the Widow Jones. She happily succumbs to his passion, and they kiss for fifteen seconds. Then the movie ends. The film was long enough to outrage a number of spectators, who viewed the kiss as pornographic. In Ottawa, Canada, calls for police intervention went unanswered (yes, there were actual calls for police intervention). One critic railed that Irwin and Rice's kiss onstage was

THE FIRST BIG-SCREEN KISS.

hard enough on the eyes (this couple was no Brad Pitt/ Jennifer Aniston)—but blowing it up to the size of a wall was pure torture. You can watch the film and judge for yourself at the Library of Congress Web site.

Opa! Let the Kissing Begin!

Greeks are passionate about food, wine, music, and dance, so it should be no surprise that kissing as we know it flourished in the Old World. The ancient Greeks not only greeted each other with kisses, they kissed their gods hello and good-bye, too. The good pagan would get up in the morning and throw a kiss to Helios, god of the sun; at night he would throw one to Hesperus, god of the evening star. When entering a temple, the devout would fling a kiss to the appropriate god; upon leaving, he or she would toss a good-bye kiss. Subjects kissed the knees of their king as a sign of subservience, slaves kissed objects belonging to their master as a show of respect, and mourners kissed the corpse at a funeral.

Stardate 5784.0: Television's First Interracial Kiss

In the *Star Trek* episode "Plato's Stepchildren" (November 22, 1968), Captain Kirk (William Shatner) and Lieutenant Uhura (Nichelle Nichols) engaged in not-too-platonic behavior by sharing TV's first interracial kiss. The ever-playful Shatner kept whispering things during filming to make Nichols laugh, forcing retakes and, thus, more kissing. According to Nichols's autobiography, they needed thirty-six takes to get the scene right.

In a 1991 interview, *Star Trek* creator Gene Roddenberry looked back on the episode and remarked, "I never considered it a big thing . . . Captain Kirk and Lieutenant Uhura's kiss was an integral part of the story line, and it never occurred to me to question whether Kirk should kiss a black person or not. I had, by that time, achieved a certain clarity about those things."

Others were not so tolerant. Many television stations in the South refused to air the episode (despite the fact that the kiss was more implied than actually shown—Kirk keeps his back to the camera during the entire smooch). And the BBC kept this episode out of syndication for nearly twenty years.

Kirk (left) and Uhura boldly go where no couple had gone before.

Interesting footnote: Later in the same episode, Vulcan half-breed Mr. Spock (Leonard Nimoy) plants a wet one on the lips of Nurse Chapel (Majel Barrett) in what is probably television's first *interspecies* kiss.

HALITOSIANS, REJOICE!

Bad breath is easily fixable thanks to sugarless gum, tongue scrapers, and bacteria-destroying toothpaste; *knowing* you have bad breath is the key. Thanks to a company called Tanita, folks in Japan no longer have to cup their hands over their mouths to check for bad breath. Instead, Tanita offers a handheld electronic gadget called the Fresh Kiss HC-201. Would-be kissers breathe into one end, and an analysis flashes upon its LCD screen—anything from "Undetectable" to "Very Bad Halitosis." The device sold a whopping 800,000 units in its first year.

Avec Langue

People were "French kissing" long before the French came along. So why do the world's biggest Jerry Lewis fans end up with all the credit?

Sadly, we have only ourselves to blame.

One definition for "French" offered by the *Oxford English Dictionary* is "spiciness." During the eighteenth century, French literature was notorious for being—in a word—dirty. Authors were writing overtly scandalous books like *Dangerous Liaisons* (1782), and the English-speaking world couldn't get enough of them. Little wonder that anything French was soon perceived as carnal or profane; phrases like "pardon my French" (cursing), "the French way" (oral sex), and "French letters" (condoms) entered the vernacular along with "French kiss."

Alfred Wolfram kissed 8,001 people in approximately eight hours in September 1990 at the Minnesota Renaissance Festival.

Playing Post Office

Children see, children do. That's the accepted maxim of many children's folklore scholars, or "childlorists"—those people who study the origins and meanings of the rhymes, games, and songs of young people.

One such childlorist—Alice Bertha Gomme—observed that "[w]hen [children] saw a custom . . . practiced with some degree of ceremonial importance, they would . . . act in play what their elders do seriously." Few things are more "ceremonial" and routine than a daily visit from a postal employee. So it's no wonder that Post Office is one of the classic children's kissing games.

The specific "rules" of Post Office vary. In one variation, a "postman" will stand outside the room and announce that another of the players has "mail." He'll also state the amount of "postage due"—that is, the number of kisses he needs to collect before turning over the mail. After the kissing

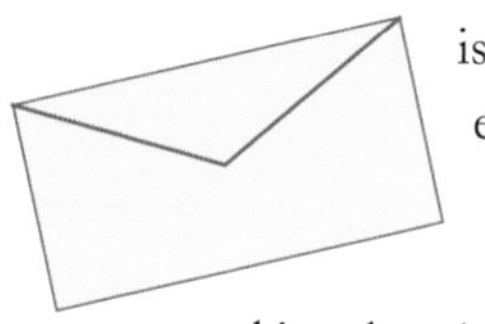

is over and the mail successfully delivered, the chosen player becomes the new postman and the game continues until everybody (hopefully) gets a kiss. Another way to play is for the postman to write a number down and send a messenger out with it. The first person to guess the number gets to smooch.

In his book *The Folkgames of Children*, Brian Sutton-Smith points out the interesting fact that over the approximately one hundred years that folklorists have been chronicling Post Office, it's changed mainly from a game in which the kissee is specifically chosen (as in the former routine above) to a game of chance (as in the latter).

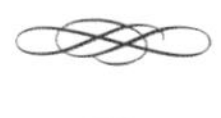

"It's a job—someone's gotta do it. The reality is, Jennifer and I can do our job well because we truly are friends. But when the day's over, she goes home to her boyfriend and I go home to a magazine."

—Actor David Schwimmer on kissing *Friends* costar Jennifer Aniston

Playing with Dolls

Admit it: You still want to play dress-up with your Barbie. If she left your parents' house via Hefty bag many years ago, the next best thing is to turn on your computer and make yourself a KiSS doll.

It's derived from a popular Japanese pastime called *Kisekae ningyou* (roughly, "clothes-changing game") in which children dress paper dolls in different colors. In the early nineties, an enterprising computer programmer developed a platform called KiSS (Kisekae Set System) that allowed users to design these paper dolls on a computer. All you need is an eye for fashion and you're ready to go.

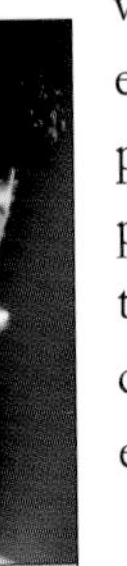

Kiss and dress up.

Part of its popularity may be that the KiSS program can be downloaded for free. KiSS-doll cyber communities have proliferated. Doll-making contests are ubiquitous. KiSS chat rooms abound. Avatars are everywhere. But even in this era of amazing technology, Mattel manages to sell one Barbie doll every three seconds. She's still the doll that everyone wants to dress.

A Killer Kiss

In early 1900s Hungary, the deadliest kiss was a living person—Bela Kiss. This middle-aged tinsmith was reputed to be quite a ladies' man; nosy neighbors often observed young women visiting his rented house in Budapest. In 1914, after Kiss was drafted to fight in World War I, his landlord visited the property to prepare it for the next tenant. He was surprised to find a number of tin drums in the yard. When he punctured one of them, the rancid smell that came out made him suspicious. It turned out that each drum contained the body of a woman, preserved in alcohol, along with the length of rope used to kill her.

Further investigations turned up additional bodies buried in the yard. Kiss had killed nearly thirty women. His MO was to take out ads in the paper—"good-looking bachelor seeks wife"—and answer only responses from women of means, whom he would bilk of their savings. If any of them became suspicious of his intentions, Kiss would do away with them. Police learned that in one instance, Kiss had forced a woman to write a letter to her mother explaining that she was so overwrought with being rejected by the great and handsome Bela Kiss, she was leaving for America to start a new life. Kiss then strangled the woman.

When authorities tried to find Kiss on the battlefront, the trail led to a Serbian hospital where their suspect was reportedly recovering from wounds. When they arrived at his bedside, the man in the bed wasn't Kiss—and he was dead. More leads poured in over the years. In 1920, police were sure they had their man, a member of the French Foreign Legion going by the name Hoffman. When they arrived at his unit, "Hoffman" had mysteriously deserted. In 1932, a New York City detective nicknamed "Camera Eye" (due to his amazing memory of faces) was convinced he spotted Kiss in Times Square, but the crowd was so large, he lost his suspect. Four years later, New York City police learned that Kiss was purportedly working as a janitor in an apartment building. Again, the suspect suddenly vanished when they arrived at the scene.

Only a handful of World War I veterans are alive today, and given Bela's relatively old age at the time of his conscription, you're probably safe from the Kiss of Death. But if you're a wealthy woman and a Hungarian guy in his early hundreds proposes to you, we would suggest you call the cops.

Thankfully, not all men by the name of Kiss have been killers. At least one Kiss did his share of improving the human condition. In Brooklyn in 1906, Max Kiss invented the first tasty laxative, Ex-Lax, relieving the world of a stubborn problem.

"A kiss without a mustache is like an egg without salt."
—Spanish proverb

Pretty Woman

Julia Roberts's kisser is worth millions, but her kissing could use some work. Or so says Dominic West, who shared a kiss with Roberts in the movie *Mona Lisa Smile*. He reported that, if pressed to rate her kissing talents, he would give her a six out of ten. Not too good. West went easy on the leading lady, though, saying that he believed her lack of passion on screen might have had something to do with her off-screen passion for her cameraman husband, who happened to be working on the set and keeping an eye on his wife.

INDIA'S ANCIENT "HOW-TO"

What we know today as French kissing probably originated in India—or so said Vaughn Bryant, a Texas A&M University anthropologist and an expert on the history of kissing, in a 1998 *Chicago Tribune* article. Having studied ancient tablets, cave art, and written documentation, Bryant was unable to find any hint of a serious make-out session prior to 1500 B.C.E. in India.

THE FIRST FRENCH KISS?

It should be no surprise, then, that the inventors of tongue slapping would produce a sex manual like the world-famous *Kama Sutra* (Aphorisms on Love), a graphic, scientific look at nearly every possibility when it comes to sex, written somewhere between the first and sixth centuries C.E. Kissing, of course, has its own special section.

"It is said by some that there is no fixed time or order between the embrace, the kiss, and the pressing or scratching with the nails or fingers, but that all these things should be done generally before sexual union takes place, while striking and making the various sounds generally takes place at the time of the union."

According to *Kama Sutra* author Vatsyayana, a respectable person is allowed to kiss the forehead, eyes, cheek, throat, breasts, lips, and inside the mouth. The "joints of the thigh," arms, and navel, however, are off limits (because that would just be crass).

Vatsyayana also defines the three different types of kisses "for a young girl": the nominal kiss, in which lips are touched, but nothing else; the throbbing kiss, in which the female moves the bottom lip but nothing else; and the touching kiss, in which the female touches her partner's lips with her tongue and takes hold of his hands.

Perhaps Vatsyayana's most noteworthy idea is his encouragement to lay a wager on who can grab hold of the other's lip in his or her teeth first—the kissing version of thumb wrestling. He instructs women on how to act if they lose ("pretend to cry") or win ("deride him, dance about . . . moving her eyebrows and rolling her eyes"). Apparently many a Bollywood movie producer has read through these instructions.

Kama Sutra Definitions

Give these kisses a try!

- In a *straight kiss*, the lovers' lips make direct contact.
- A kiss that occurs with the partners' heads bent toward each other is a *bent kiss*.
- For a *turned kiss*, one lover holds the other's head and chin, turning up the partner's face.
- Giving a lover's lower lip a forceful press makes a *pressed kiss*.
- The *greatly pressed kiss* goes a step further. One partner starts by grasping the other's lower lip between two fingers. The first lover touches their tongue to the other's lip and then presses his or her own lip forcefully against their partner's. See how your beloved responds to that one.

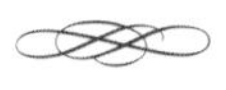

"Kiss the children for me and a hundred for yourself."

—Ulysses S. Grant,
in a letter to his wife Julia

Richard Dawson's Love Connection

The man who coined the immortal words "Survey says!" on the hit game show *Family Feud* was also famous for greeting every weak-kneed female contestant with a kiss (usually on the cheek). These amorous antics earned Dawson $3.5 million a year, an Emmy Award, and plenty of ridicule; in one classic *Saturday Night Live* sketch, Dawson (played by Bill Murray) offers to French kiss a member of the Conehead family.

Johnson (left) and Dawson (right) share a smooch.

But in the end, all of Dawson's kissing paid off. On April 6, 1981, the Johnson Clan appeared on *Family Feud*. And when Dawson's lips met those of Gretchen Johnson, sparks flew. The two fell in love, married in 1991, and—aside from the occasional feud that all couples experience—remain happily wedded to this day.

Kissing for a Cause

In November 2003, River Hill High School junior Stephanie Haaser stepped up on a table in her Clarksville, Maryland, cafeteria, bellowed, "End homophobia, now!" and then made out with her friend Katherine Pecore in front of the student body for approximately twelve seconds. Haaser mistakenly interpreted the eruption of applause and cheering following the kiss as support for her cause.

The gals said their kiss was inspired by an English teacher who urged his students to commit a "nonconformist" act, just like the great American writers Henry David Thoreau and Ralph Waldo Emerson. All the girls received for completing their assignment was two days of suspension—although Haaser also earned a spot on ABC's *Good Morning America*, where, after asserting her heterosexuality, said she had no regrets and would suck face with her friend all over again.

Reaction from the community was mixed. Some called the suspension a witch hunt. Others wanted to see Haaser and Pecore burned at the stake. River Hill principal Scott Pfeifer, who presides over a school that observes National Coming Out Day, was steadfast. "I'm confident I made the right decision," he said in a *Washington Post* interview. "Anybody who would stand up and do a disruptive act, I would treat them the same way." He added that he did respect the gals' chutzpah.

And their legacy lives on, sort of. River Hill students inspired by the cafeteria spectacle later organized an anti-homophobia rally. The *Washington Post* reported two people in attendance.

"I think I'm still clean-living. I mean, I don't go home and have orgies or anything like that."

—Britney Spears to CNN, in the aftermath of her infamous three-way kiss with Madonna and Christina Aguilera at the 2003 MTV Video Music Awards

The Kiss, Then and Now

"One has the impression of seeing the delight of this kiss all over these bodies; it is like a sun which rises and its light is everywhere." So said the poet Rainer Maria Rilke of this legendary masterpiece, created by Auguste Rodin near the end of the nineteenth century as part of a much larger sculpture called the *Gates of Hell*.

The two lovers were inspired by Paolo and Francesca, two characters from Dante's *Divine Comedy*, but Rodin later decided that their joy seemed out of place with the rest of his composition. He eventually removed his lovers from the sculpture and began exhibiting them as an independent work. Critics dubbed the sculpture *The Kiss*, and the response from the public was overwhelming. Yet Rodin himself acted like it was all no big deal. "It is a big ornament," he sniffed, "sculpted according to the usual formula and which focuses attention on the two personages instead of opening up wide horizons to daydreams."

Ornamental or not, *The Kiss* astonished art lovers and scared the wits out of puritans. When a three-ton copy was put on public display in the English town of Lewes in 1914, a local headmistress named Miss Fowler-Tutt strongly objected. As she saw it, the town was packed with soldiers

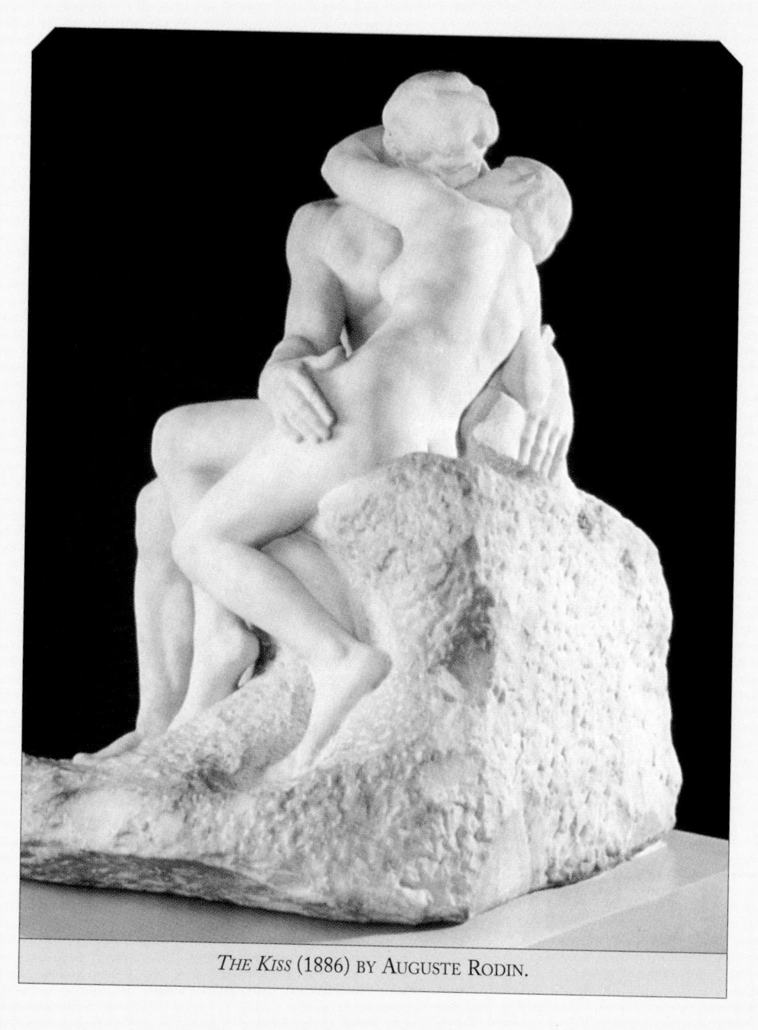

The Kiss (1886) by Auguste Rodin.

waiting to head to the war front, and it wasn't a good idea to put kissing on their minds. The sculpture was covered with a piece of canvas and later removed from view.

Nearly a century later, it was shrouded again (albeit partially) because contemporary British artist Cornelia Parker decided that *The Kiss* wasn't erotic *enough*. Parker had already achieved some notoriety for such artistic achievements as exploding a garden shed filled with junk. With permission of the Tate Britain Gallery, she wrapped a mile-long piece of string around Rodin's sculpture and deemed the new work *The Distance (A Kiss with String Attached)*. In an interview with the *Times* (UK), Parker said she tied the string most tightly around the mouths of the figures "because it is in the kiss that there is most tension. But the binding starts to relax as they become more informal, gradually unraveling as it falls around their bodies."

According to a Tate Gallery spokesperson, Parker revived the sculpture's punch by "mak[ing] you think about how [the lovers'] heads are bound together and the claustrophobia of relationships, what it's like to be bound to someone else." Others felt that Parker had simply tied a lot of string around a really nice statue.

No sooner had the pair of lovers been tied together

than a thirty-six-year-old man used a pair of scissors to express *his* personal view of Parker's art. It wasn't clear whether he considered his act of string-snipping an art form, or if he was just pissed off. Nevertheless, he was quickly detained by authorities, and Parker, unfazed, bound the kissers up once again.

A Macabre Kiss of Death

At least Cornelia Parker has a sense of humor—an exploding garden shed is pretty funny, no matter how you slice it. A dead man's head, though, is not usually funny, *especially* if you slice it. New Mexico photographer Joel-Peter Witkin takes *his* craft to the farthest reaches of grisliness. One of his most controversial and famous works is *The Kiss*, a photo of an old man's head cleaved in two and positioned face to face, so it looks like he's kissing himself. ("It's a pity I can't kiss myself," Sigmund Freud once wrote; if only he were alive today.)

Witkin claims he likes to make his audiences face the grim reality of death (apparently he doesn't watch cable news or read newspapers much). Revered by many in the art world, Witkin has received tens of thousands of dollars in grants from the National Endowment for the Arts for creating works that are shocking and impossible to ignore, including a photo of a headless corpse sitting in a chair.

Kissing *Can* Lead to Pregnancy!

In the case of birds, anyway. Most male birds have no exterior sex organ, so they can't impregnate females in a manner that most people are familiar with. The male does produce sperm in his testes, however, and that sperm is sent to a cavity near the posterior orifice called the *cloaca*. There it remains until mating season, when the male's testicles grow to hundreds of times their original size. When the mood strikes, the female will move her tail aside, allowing the male to press his cloaca against hers. At this moment, the sperm literally jumps out of the male's cloaca and into the female's, then swims for dear life up the oviduct to the ovum. The zoological term for the pressing of cloacas is the "cloacal kiss."

Locking Lips Along the Nile

The stiff-jointed figures of Egyptian art make the denizens of North Africa's ancient civilization look staid at best—certainly not the sorts to express themselves through passionate kissing. But if you look at a short-lived period of Egypt's history, you'll see images of a pharaoh who not only has flexible joints, but lips to go along with them.

Akhenaton, who ruled the kingdom during the fourteenth century B.C.E., instructed his royal sculptors to chisel exactly what they saw—no more stiff representations, no more arms bent at ninety-degree angles. One of the most famous works from this period is a relief carving that shows the royal family grouped together—all eight of them—hugging and kissing. In another unfinished piece, Akhenaton is tenderly kissing his daughter—a proud dad doting over his little girl.

When the pharaoh died, conservatives set themselves to the task of destroying all the artwork created during Akhenaton's rule. It's the reason we don't see more realistic displays of affection in Egyptian art. But don't be fooled by that stoic sphinx. Many a person has smooched right under its (now-missing) nose.

Keep Your Tongue in Your Mouth!

Parents no longer attempt to keep kids chaste by telling them that kissing can lead to pregnancy—but they still don't want teenagers making out in the schoolyard.

A joint 2004 poll conducted by National Public Radio, the Kaiser Family Foundation, and Harvard's Kennedy School of Government asked parents of high school students if they agreed or disagreed with the following statement: "Abstinence from sexual activity outside marriage is the expected standard for all school-age children." According to 65 percent of the respondents, the statement was right on target.

Passionate kissing?

The poll then asked these parents to clarify what constituted "sexual activity," and 63 percent said kids shouldn't take part in "intimate touching"; another 44 percent said the same about masturbation. As far as "passionate kissing" goes, a whopping 42 percent gave the thumbs-down.

A Mouth Full of Blarney

All year, every year, Americans wearing kelly-green "Kiss Me, I'm Irish" sweatshirts flock to County Cork to kiss the famous Blarney Stone. Legend claims that when you press your lips to the famous stone, you magically gain the ability to tell lies like an Irishman.

Some claim the stone is half of the Stone of Scone, a rock once used by Jacob as a pillow, and originally the property of Scotland; in centuries past, budding Scottish kings would be crowned over the stone. In 1314, as one version of the story goes, a Scot named Robert the Bruce (the guy from *Braveheart* who turns on the English at the end) offered half the stone to the McCarthy family of Ireland for their support against the English at the Battle of Bannockburn.

Fast forward another two hundred years or so to the reign of England's Queen Elizabeth I. She found herself frustrated with a fellow named Cormac McCarthy, then lord of Blarney. He would frequently profess his devotion to the queen, but refused to ever admit that his land belonged to England. Eventually, the queen lost her patience and declared that McCarthy was just giving her a lot of "blarney."

It's now believed that if you visit Blarney Castle and kiss the stone, you will obtain Lord Cormac McCarthy's special talent. But you may want to think twice before puckering up: It's been said that Blarney locals will sometimes "water the rock" after a long night of drinking pints of Guinness.

BEST JOKE ABOUT THE BLARNEY STONE

A busload of tourists in Ireland go to see the Blarney Stone. When they arrive, the site is closed because the stone is being cleaned. The Irish tour guide apologizes and explains that according to legend, those who kiss the Blarney Stone will have good luck the rest of their lives.

A cranky tourist says, "Oh, that's just great. What a lousy trip. We won't be here tomorrow, so I guess we can't kiss the stone."

The tour guide then politely informs her that there's another way to get the good luck: You can kiss someone who *has* kissed the Blarney Stone, and the luck will be transferred from their lips to yours.

"Oh, and I suppose you've kissed it," the woman scowls. "No, ma'am," the tour guide replies, "but I have sat on it."

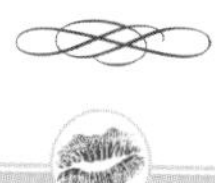

"There's nothing like a kiss long and hot down to your soul that almost paralyzes you. . . ."

—Molly Bloom in the novel *Ulysses* by James Joyce

KEEP IT SIMPLE, STUPID (K.I.S.S.)

This popular catchphrase was purportedly coined by a man who developed the most technologically complex aircraft of its kind—the U-2 spy plane. Clarence Leonard "Kelly" Johnson, a designer at defense contractor Lockheed's super-secret "Skunk Works" factory, made the phrase his trademark expression during the 1950s. It must be easy for engineers to forget this simple maxim when they're dealing with things like phugoid oscillation, translational motion, and computational fluid dynamics.

Kissing Cocktails

Bee's Kiss

1 $^{1}/_{2}$ oz. (45 ml) light rum
1 oz. (30 ml) heavy cream
1 tsp. (5 ml) honey
Freshly grated nutmeg

Shake the ingredients well with ice; then strain into a chilled cocktail glass. Dust with nutmeg.

French Kiss

$^{1}/_{2}$ oz. (15 ml) Grand Marnier
1 oz. (30 ml) raspberry liqueur
1 oz. (30 ml) whipping cream
1 oz. (30 ml) vodka
Fresh raspberry

Combine the ingredients and shake with crushed ice. Strain into a champagne flute. Add a raspberry for garnish, and enjoy.

Midnight Kiss

$^{3}/_{4}$ oz. (22 ml) Smirnoff vodka
6–8 oz. (180–240 ml) champagne
Dash of blue curaçao
White or gold sugar

Pour the vodka into a champagne flute. Fill glass with champagne. Top with blue curaçao. For extra razzle-dazzle, give the flute a sugar rim before filling.

Satan's Kiss

$1^1/_2$ oz. (45 ml) Seagram's VO Canadian Whisky
1 12-oz. (355-ml) can raspberry lemonade
(from frozen concentrate)
Splash of lemon-lime soda
Lime wedge

Pour the whisky into a rocks glass. Fill with raspberry lemonade. Add a splash of lemon-lime soda. Squeeze a lime wedge into the mix, and add as garnish.

Sicilian Kiss

$1^1/_2$ oz. (45 ml) Southern Comfort
$^3/_4$ oz. (22 ml) amaretto

Pour over ice in large rocks glass.

Soul Kiss

$^3/_4$ oz. (22 ml) dry vermouth
$1^1/_2$ tsp. (7.5 ml) Dubonnet
$^3/_4$ oz. (22 ml) bourbon whiskey
$1^1/_2$ tsp. (7.5 ml) orange juice

Shake all ingredients with ice and strain into cocktail glass.

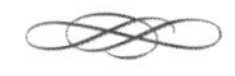

Dr. Martin Luther King Jr. receives a kiss from his wife, Coretta Scott King, following his 1965 conviction for leading an illegal boycott of segregated buses.

KEEP YOUR LIPS TO YOURSELF!

The practice of kissing hello is called *beso-beso* in the Philippines. Well, in the summer of '04 the country's president, Gloria Macapagal-Arroyo, decided that she had had it up to here with beso-beso. While visiting Filipino workers in Kuwait, Macapagal-Arroyo's bodyguards jostled with a would-be kisser, whose mid-pucker mug was plastered all over the papers the following day. Macapagal-Arroyo made an announcement declaring that the only kisses she would accept would come from her husband. "Please, all the men in the country, so that I won't be rude to you, do not attempt to kiss me," the president cautioned.

The Philippine city of Manila holds the record for the most people simultaneously kissing. On Valentine's Day 2004, 5,327 couples puckered up at the stroke of midnight and kissed each other for ten seconds at the city's Lovapalooza Festival.

KISSING COUSINS

Apes have a lot in common with humans. They play with toys, dote over pets, fight with their fists, and eat bananas. Believe it or not, they also kiss and make up. Several species of primates have been witnessed in the wild using body contact as a sign of peacemaking. After a quarrel, they'll occasionally approach one another to offer a hug and a kiss. Chimpanzees, stump-tailed monkeys, and rhesus monkeys all make up with a good make-out session.

MONKEYING AROUND.

But no ape kisses seem quite as human as those of the bonobo. The most sexually active of all primates, the bonobo is evolutionarily as close to the human, if not closer, than the chimpanzee. Not only does this ape "French kiss" for the sheer pleasure of the act, it's also the only primate (besides the human) to copulate face to face. But that's a topic for a different book.

Top Ten Kissing Songs of the 1980s

1. "Kiss" by Prince and the Revolution
2. "Kiss" by The Art of Noise featuring Tom Jones
3. "Kiss on My List" by Hall & Oates
4. "Kissing a Fool" by George Michael
5. "Kiss of Life" by Peter Gabriel
6. "French Kissin' in the USA" by Debbie Harry
7. "Kiss Off" by Violent Femmes
8. "The Perfect Kiss" by New Order
9. "Kiss Me Deadly" by Lita Ford
10. "Kissability" by Sonic Youth

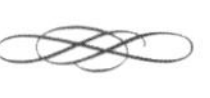

"In protest of France's opposition to a U.S. war on Iraq, the U.S. Congress's cafeteria has changed french fries and french toast to 'freedom fries' and 'freedom toast.' Afterwards, the congressmen were so pleased with themselves, they all started freedom kissing each other."

—Tina Fey, reporting the "news" on *Saturday Night Live*

Kissing Etymology

Kiss Black Betty (eighteenth century): to be drunk. Attributed to Ben Franklin. A "Black Betty" was a liquor bottle made of dark glass.

Kiss the Gunner's Daughter (eighteenth century): to be flogged. When sailors were whipped, they would often be tied, face down, to a cannon, which was called "the gunner's daughter."

Kiss the Baby (nineteenth century): to take a drink of liquor. Used in Great Britain and America. "Baby" used to be slang for a small bottle of liquor.

Kiss Mary (1950s): to smoke pot. Mary being a popular slang term for marijuana.

Kiss of Life (1960s): cardiopulmonary resuscitation (CPR). Austrian-American physicist Peter Safar invented the life-saving procedure by combining mouth-to-mouth resuscitation with chest compressions. Much better than the ancient practice of flogging a person until he began breathing again.

Kiss the Fish (1970s): to smoke pot or hashish. We don't get it, either.

Kissing Cultures

When traveling, it's helpful to be aware of local attitudes about kissing. Italians will offer a kiss on both cheeks, many Russians kiss three times, and the French have even been known to kiss four times. Some Arab men may greet one another with a kiss on each shoulder. Even the Japanese—who were once very shy about kissing in public—have slowly begun to adopt the Western-style kiss greeting. But China is still holding out. Travel guides intended for Western audiences always advise against greeting a Chinese person with a kiss (to play it safe, wait for them to make the first move; you'll either nod, bow, or shake hands). And if you're traveling in Iran, you don't even want to think about kissing someone in public. Read on if you want to know why.

Kiss This, Council of Guardians!

Channel surf for ten minutes and you're guaranteed to stumble across at least one award ceremony in which famous people are giving themselves laurels for being famous. The amount of self-congratulatory kissing that goes on at these things is ridiculous. That is, of course, if the event occurs in a Western nation. In other parts of the world, a public kiss can get even the rich and famous in big trouble.

In a September 2002 film award ceremony held in the Iranian city of Yazd, actress Gohar Kheirandish announced the winner for best filmmaker, Ali Zamini. Kheirandish, a beautiful woman in her fifties, was so happy for Zamini that when he came on stage, she kissed him on his forehead, much like a doting mother would kiss her child for winning a spelling bee. Zamini is, in fact, about thirty years younger than Kheirandish—but the law is the law. In Iran, men and women are legally forbidden to show any affection in public. The filmmaker was arrested for *receiving* the kiss and then released after paying the equivalent of $2,500 bail; the actress was arrested by Iran's culture police and sentenced to a flogging of seventy-four lashes. In case you're not familiar with this practice, the recipient of an Iranian flogging is tied to a tree (usually in a public place), stripped to the waist, and whipped with a leather strap. The public humiliation is almost as bad as the bloody welts. After Kheirandish publicly apologized, the sentence was suspended—with a caveat: Let your lips get the best of you again and the countdown begins.

One grouchy editor from the Iranian newspaper *Ya Lesarat* (a mouthpiece of Iran's ultraconservative Council of Guardians) carped, "Our enemies are trying to harm Islam through our culture and this event is an example of that fact." All this fuss over a little kiss on the forehead. Here's some advice for all of you smooching Hollywood celebrities: Keep your kisses stateside.

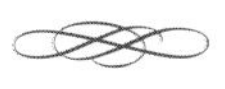

"No, I don't think I will kiss you, although you need kissing, badly. That's what's wrong with you. You should be kissed and often, and by someone who knows how."

—Rhett Butler (Clark Gable)
to Scarlett O'Hara (Vivien Leigh)
in *Gone With the Wind*

Teaching Abstinence, Circa 420 B.C.E.

Socrates was no fan of normal human emotion; he believed it led inevitably to a lack of self-control. In his book *Memorabilia*, an account of the life and teachings of Socrates, Xenophon describes a scene in which Socrates sums up his view of kissing. Socrates berates two students—Critobulus and Xenophon himself—when it's revealed that Critobulus had recently enjoyed a kiss. Socrates, aghast at the act, describes Critobulus as hotheaded and reckless: "This is the sort of man to throw somersaults into knives, or to leap into the jaws of fire."

Xenophon comes to the defense of his friend. He says that kissing sounds enjoyable, to which Socrates replies: "Don't you realize that you would instantly be a slave instead of a free man, and spend a lot of money on harmful pleasures, and have no time to take an interest in anything truly good, and be forced to exert yourself for ends that not even a lunatic would bother about?"

Digging his hole deeper, Xenophon tells Socrates that

he's making much too much about a simple little kiss. Pshaw, says Socrates, who then goes on to compare a beauty's kiss to the bite of a spider that "drives one crazy." The teacher gives his students a bit of advice: "I advise you, Xenophon, when you see an attractive person, to take to your heels as fast as you can; and I advise you, Critobulus, to go away for a year. That may give you just enough time to recover."

BIZARRE KISSING LAW #3: Wisconsin

Taking the train from Chicago to Madison? Put your lips away when you cross the state line, because kissing on a train in Wisconsin is expressly forbidden.

How to Avoid Bumping Noses

When initiating a first kiss, 66 percent of people turn their heads to the right. (If everyone on the receiving end did the same, there'd be a lot less embarrassment in the world!)

WORN DOWN BY THE LIPS OF TIME

How many kisses does it take to wear through 1.5 inches of bronze? The answer is anyone's guess, but a statue of St. Peter in Rome proves that the hardy metal is no match for millions of Catholic lips. So many pilgrims have devoutly kissed the foot of the statue in St. Peter's Basilica that the front of the poor saint's foot is almost completely worn down.

POPE JOHN XXIII ON JUNE 28, 1960, THE FEAST DAY OF ST. PETER.

No one is quite sure when the statue was cast. Some estimate that it was created in the thirteenth century; others maintain that the statue dates back to the fifth or sixth century. And there are those who insist the statue of St. Peter is not a statue of St. Peter at all. They maintain it's actually the likeness of Jupiter, dating back to pre-Christian Rome. If this is the case, millions of Catholic pilgrims have been mistakenly kissing the foot of a pagan god. But, as they say: Once given, a kiss can't be taken back.

KISS THE SKULL

Many of the world's wealthiest power brokers (and more than a few U.S. presidents) have shared a common experience in the past—namely, membership in Skull and Bones, the secret fraternity of Yale University. Only the fraternity became not so secret when a *New York Observer* reporter and a team of spies equipped with high-tech microphones and night-vision cameras caught the group's bizarre initiation ceremony on tape. It was subsequently aired on news stations across America.

The ceremony resembled something between a medieval witch rite, a homoerotic frat party, and the climax of *Lord of the Flies*. America's future political and industry leaders were dressed in togas, acting out murders, and masquerading as George W. Bush. Members chanted, "Kiss the skull! Kiss the skull!" while initiates knelt to kiss a sacred skull that was placed on the ground. Then a man dressed as the Pope arrived, and the newbies knelt to kiss his slipper. One wonders what evangelical supporters of a certain Skull and Bones member/president might say about the fact that their guy has conceivably "bowed to Rome."

Kissing the Closet Good-Bye

At some point in the mid-1990s, television producers must have realized that a good percentage of their viewing audience enjoys watching women make out. And so recent U.S. television history has seen a rash of girl-on-girl kisses. The *Relativity* Kiss. The *Roseanne* Kiss. The *Ally McBeal* Kiss. The Madonna-Britney-Christina Kiss. The *Buffy* Kiss. The *All My Children* Kiss.

And then there's Ellen DeGeneres. The comedian made television history in April 1997 when she famously kissed the closet good-bye on her ABC sitcom *Ellen*. But the episode doesn't feature any actual smooching; Ellen's character merely mentions that she happens to like girls. The episode earned the highest ratings the sitcom

Ellen's coming-out party.

had ever seen, along with an Emmy award.

And the following season, when Ellen's character finally did kiss a female friend—an essentially nonsexual smooch designed primarly for comedy relief—ABC prefaced the episode with an "adult content" warning. DeGeneres objected, reminding ABC execs that several successful sitcoms, including *Spin City* and *The Drew Carey Show*, had already featured man-to-man kisses (unfortunately, these examples were all designed to poke fun at homosexuality, not to offer a realistic portrayal). In the end, ABC dropped the warnings. But given threatened advertiser boycotts after the "outing" episode, strained relations with its star, and the perception that audiences were getting tired of a sitcom about a lesbian bookstore owner, the network decided that Ellen had overstayed its welcome. The show was canceled after its fifth season.

"Know what Paul and I are doing for our season finale? A lesbian kiss."

—David Letterman

THE KISS (1897) BY EDVARD MUNCH.

SOMETHING FISHY

Let's review what we've learned so far: People kiss. Apes kiss. Even birds kiss, sort of. But what about fish? Is it true that certain fish kiss?

In a sense, yes. Consider the *Helostoma temminckii*, a freshwater tropical fish indigenous to Southeast Asia but popular with aquarium hobbyists around the world. What makes this fish special is that it regularly lives up to its nickname—the "kissing gourami."

From time to time, two male gourami will approach one another, lock lips, and proceed to "kiss"—often for several minutes at a time. Don't mistake this for a moment of intimacy. These kissers are actually lip-locked in a test of strength to impress the best-looking gals—and to earn rights to the best spots in the tank. The loser of the match (the fish that pulls away first) retreats to a corner of the tank; the winner sometimes hunts him down and kills him.

"People who throw kisses are hopelessly lazy."

—Bob Hope

KISS YOUR SINS GOOD-BYE

Every year beginning sometime in January or February, the world's greatest kissing event occurs in Saudi Arabia's holy city of Mecca. As part of their pilgrimage called *hajj*, millions of Muslims travel to the Kaaba—Islam's most sacred temple and the place Muslims face when they pray (regardless of where they happen to be in the world). It's here that they kiss the Kaaba's eastern cornerstone—called the Black Stone—which was reportedly placed by the temple's builders, Abraham and his son Ishmael.

THE KAABA WITHIN THE GRAND MOSQUE.

It's also believed by some that the Black Stone was originally pure white but turned black from absorbing sinners' kisses over the past 1,500 years. On the Day of Judgment, some expect that Allah will bring forth the stone (which will have grown eyes and a tongue) to pick out the righteous to tell them "job well done."

Until then, devout Muslims throng around the temple and attempt to kiss the Black Stone, just as their prophet Muhammad did back in the seventh century. It's pretty much a free-for-all—and with millions of people showing up, many never get close enough to kiss the Black Stone. Some perform the ritual by reaching out and touching it, then kissing their hand; if they're more than an arm's reach away, they can use an object, like a broom handle or baseball bat, to touch the stone and then kiss the object. If a person is *really* far away, he or she can simply point at the stone. Perhaps an online virtual kiss via Mecca-cam will be next.

"I know that you are but a stone, incapable of doing good or harm. Had I not seen the Messenger of God kiss you . . . I would not kiss you."

—Caliph Umar ibn al-Khattab,
companion of the Prophet Muhammad

Fraternizing with the Troops

The Scottish clan Gordon has always been known as a scrappy crowd, constantly fighting with rival clans beginning in the eleventh century. But fighters can also be lovers, and sometimes the two go hand in hand.

Make love, then war.

Back in late eighteenth-century Scotland, the leader of a region would raise armies as needed as a service to his king. At that time, relations between Great Britain and America were still pretty testy (this was just after the American Revolution, of course). King George wanted more soldiers, and the Scottish Duke of Gordon was running low on recruits. Fortunately, the Duchess of Gordon came up with a perfect (and rather intimate) solution.

In a brilliant PR stunt, she announced that each man who volunteered to join up would receive a shilling, transacted mouth-to-mouth through a kiss from the duchess.

Men in kilts showed up in droves for a snog and a shilling, and the 2nd Battalion of the Gordon Highlanders was born.

A Kiss and a Crush

If you're dating a West Point cadet and he suggests an innocent stroll about the campus, be careful. He might take you along "Flirtation Walk," lead you underneath a big rock, and demand a kiss. Which puts you in a very difficult position. According to legend, if a gal refuses a kiss underneath the stone outcropping called Kissing Rock, the stone will fall and squash her. There's even a song called "By the Kissing Rock" in the 1950 movie *The West Point Story*, starring James Cagney and Doris Day, that chronicles the demise of a girl too prudish for her own good.

BIZARRE KISSING LAW #4: Iowa

Apparently, cops in the Hawkeye State are armed with stopwatches. Kisses in Iowa must not last longer than five minutes.

Under the Mistletoe

Too much eggnog, idiotic dancing, and after-hours antics in the copy room all make for good office Christmas parties. But they're never a complete success without a nice, juicy mistletoe scandal.

As with many Christmas customs, the origins of mistletoe date back hundreds of years to the north European pagans. Long before the first holiday party was planned, people from Iceland to Sweden to England were pressing lips under mistletoe, and it wasn't to keep warm. In Norse mythology, the all-seeing goddess Frigg foresaw the imminent death of her son Balder. In order to prevent it, she made all the material on earth—every hill, tree, grain of sand, you name it—vow not to harm him. But in all her mother's worrying, she overlooked mistletoe. The prankster god Loki learned of this and arranged for Balder to be killed with a spear of mistletoe, the only earthly material that could do so. Balder was eventually brought back to life, but to help mistletoe atone for its transgressions, Frigg declared it a symbol of love, not death. Everyone in northern Europe—even enemies, it's said—would embrace and kiss each other if they happened to meet in the forest under a branch of mistletoe.

Others trace the custom back to the Druids, the intelligentsia class of the ancient Celts. They considered mistletoe sacred, especially when growing on an oak tree. One can only imagine what it meant to a nature worshipper on a walk through the gray, leafless woods in December, when he stumbled upon a nice, green sprig of mistletoe, unlike other evergreens, sprouting ten feet above the ground. Gotta be magic! The Druids would solemnly gather under their holy twig and hold their sacred rituals.

The first use of mistletoe at Christmas dates back to sixteenth-century England, where one berry would be removed from the plant after each kiss. When all the berries were gone, the kissing had to cease. Thankfully, that aspect of the custom is all but extinct, allowing Christmas revelers to warm their lips throughout the season.

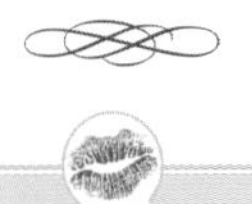

"A kiss on your heart, and one much lower down, much lower!"

—Napoleon to Josephine, in a letter attempting to convince his new wife to join him on the battlefront for a honeymoon

August 25, 1944: An American soldier gets a kiss of gratitude at the liberation of Paris.

A Good Healthy Kiss

So you're all puckered up and waiting. Then your partner says he isn't in the mood. Inform him that good kissing means good health. He can work out, strengthen his heart, and please you, all at the same time. During a passionate kiss, your neck, shoulders, mouth, arms, and tongue are all hard at work. According to one report, a good kiss burns about 2 calories per minute, or 120 per hour—twice the rate you burn while sitting there like a lump wondering if you should make your move.

And the better the kiss, the better-looking you'll remain in life. A passionate French kiss works out more than thirty facial muscles, keeping them toned to perfection. Plus, your partner's germ-ridden saliva in your mouth builds up antibodies, improving your immune system. There's simply no excuse not to kiss, unless of course you have a headache.

"I wasn't kissing her. I was whispering into her mouth."

—Chico Marx, after his wife caught him kissing a chorus girl

With This Kiss, I Thee Kill

There can't be too many things worse than getting a big kiss from some Tony Soprano wannabe in northern New Jersey—it means you're about to become fish food. Mob movies like *The Godfather* brought the "kiss of death" into the public vernacular, but the concept actually dates back to the Bible.

Perhaps the most famous example occurs in the Garden of Gethsemane, where Judas tells a group of Roman soldiers, "The one I will kiss is the man; arrest him" (Matthew 26:48). Judas then approaches Jesus with the words, "Greetings, Rabbi!" and kisses him, marking him for death. It's considered by many Christians to be the greatest sin of humankind.

JUDAS—HISTORY'S WORST KISSER.

But Judas didn't invent the kiss of death, either. In the Old Testament's second book of Samuel, we meet a military commander named Joab who finds himself replaced by a rival named Amasa. Overwrought with jealousy, Joab decides to rectify the situation: "Joab said to Amasa, 'Is it well with you my brother?' And Joab took Amasa by the beard with his right hand to kiss him. But Amasa did not notice the sword in Joab's hand; Joab struck him in the belly so that his entrails poured out on the ground, and he died" (20:9-10).

If Judas is the New Testament's John Gotti, making others do his dirty work, Joab is the Old Testament's Sammy the Bull, performing his thuggish deeds up close and personal.

But the *Original* Kiss of Death . . .

. . . comes from the Big Guy himself. According to the Talmud, a collection of ancient rabbinic writings on Jewish law and tradition, there are 903 ways to die, ranging from death by stoning to something called "God's kiss"—the former unbelievably painful, the latter unbelievably pleasant. (The Talmud leaves the remaining 901 ways of dying to our imagination.)

Only a handful of people are known to have died at the lips of God—Moses, Aaron, Miriam, and the Patriarchs. (According to the Old Testament, anyone who dies suddenly after the age of eighty has also been kissed by God.) The rest of us have to deal with the Angel of Death, in the form of croup, plague, or express bus.

The concept is traced back to two passages in Jewish scripture: "Aaron the priest ascended Mount Hor by the mouth of the Lord and died there" (Numbers 33:38) and "Moses the servant of the Lord died there in the land of Moab by the mouth of the Lord" (Deuteronomy 34:5). Talmudic scholars interpreted God's "mouth" to mean God's "kiss." The interpretation makes more sense when you put the passages into the context of ancient civilizations, which often believed that a person's breath contained his spirit or "essence" and that two people's spirits were connected through kisses.

Interestingly, the Christian New Revised Standard Version of the Bible translates the key parts in the passages as "at the command of the Lord" and "at the Lord's command": God didn't kiss them into death, according to these translators. Apparently, he just told them to die.

"Let him kiss me with the kisses of his mouth: For thy love is better than wine."

—Song of Solomon

Boys Don't Make Passes at Girls Who Wear . . . Braces?

Braces are an affliction to millions of teenagers (and plenty of older people, too). Almost as common is the belief that an open-mouthed kiss between two wearers of braces risks an embarrasing entanglement of brackets and wires, with mouths becoming difficult to separate and the situation's romance even harder to recover. But kiss expert William Cane suggests that braces can actually be considered attractive jewelry (like tongue rings) and are not a hindrance to kissing at all. Of course, his example of an attractive, orthodontically enhanced maiden was Dominique Swain's underage title character in the 1997 film *Lolita*.

Presidential Kisses

George Washington has a number of "firsts" under his belt, including one very famous presidential kiss. Inside New York City's Federal Hall on April 30, 1789, the general set a presidential standard when, after swearing his oath of office, he pressed those thin lips of his to the Bible. As the story goes, however, he *almost* didn't have a Bible to kiss. Everything for the ceremony had been planned out in excruciating detail—except for the Good Book. At the last minute, the nation's first congressmen scrambled around Federal Hall like chickens with their heads cut off, in desperate search of a Bible. Eventually, parade marshall Jacob Morton sprinted to his Masonic Lodge a block away, grabbed their copy, and hightailed it

Washington kissed here.

back to Federal Hall. "I swear, so help me God!" Washington said at the end of his oath and kissed the Masonic Bible, which remains in possession of the same Masonic Lodge to this day. Nearly one hundred years later, James Garfield would set another presidential precedent: He was the first one to kiss his wife at an inauguration.

Top Ten Kissing Songs of the 1990s

1. "Suck My Kiss" by The Red Hot Chili Peppers
2. "Kiss from a Rose" by Seal
3. "Passionate Kisses" by Mary Chapin Carpenter
4. "This Kiss" by Faith Hill
5. "Last Kiss" by Pearl Jam
6. "Kiss of Life" by Sade
7. "Kiss Them for Me" by Siouxsie and the Banshees
8. "Knock Me a Kiss" by B. B. King
9. "Butterfly Kisses" by Bob Carlisle
10. "Kiss the Flame" by Jewel

The Shot Seen 'Round the World

It's not every day when a man on the street can grab the nearest woman and kiss her on the lips—but then again, August 14, 1945, was not every day. Alfred Eisenstaedt's magical *LIFE* magazine photo (of a sailor kissing a woman in Times Square) captures the jubilation felt in America on V-J Day. It's the most reproduced photograph in the magazine's archives—but for decades, the identities of the subjects remained a mystery.

Then, in 1980, a former nurse named Edith Shain stepped forward to claim the throne. "I didn't think it was dignified [then], but times have changed," she told *LIFE*, explaining her newfound frankness. Eisenstaedt met with the sixty-two-year-old, verified she was the one, and snapped her picture a second time. After *LIFE* magazine ran a photo of Shain, more than a dozen men came forward claiming to be the sailor, each with his own claim to authenticity: "That's *my* hairline!" "That's *my* mole!" "Those are *my* hands!" Shain was skeptical. She asked each man what he had said to her after the kiss, and each impostor gave the wrong answer.

Finally, in 1995, a retired police officer named Carl "Moose" Muscarello came forth and gave the correct

Potential kissers crowd Times Square on August 14, 1945.

response: Nothing. He had said absolutely nothing. They simply kissed and went on their merry ways. In an interview with National Public Radio, Muscarello described the experience: "I just walked over and grabbed her and very gently planted a long, luscious kiss on her beautiful lips . . . and when I was out of breath I just stepped back and . . . drifted off into the crowd, ran off and kissed a few more ladies, and got on the subway and went back to my home in Brooklyn."

The Kissing Disease

For teenagers past and present, the effects of infectious mononucleosis can be worse than getting grounded. The best-known symptoms of the so-called kissing disease are several months of sleepiness, dizziness, and more sleepiness—plus sore throat, fever, and abdominal pain. In rare cases, mono can lead to a swollen spleen or liver. There is no cure.

Mono is actually caused by the Epstein-Barr virus (EBV), one of the most common of all viruses and a type of herpes simplex. According to the U.S. Centers for Disease Control, if you're infected during adolescence with EBV, you have a 35 to 50 percent chance of getting mono. Fortunately, a lot of people are exposed to EBV during childhood and develop the antibodies necessary to thwart the disease. Unfortunately, these same people become carriers of the virus and go around spreading it like the plague. The disease is famously spread by kissing, of course, but it can be transmitted by any exchange of saliva or mucus. And once you have it, the virus makes a happy home of your body for the rest of your life.

Since any number of viruses and diseases can be spread this way, one might wonder why mono is singled out in high schools across the land as "The Kissing Disease."

There are two explanations: (1) teenagers are more susceptible to mono than anyone else, and (2) teenagers are mean.

Top Ten Make-Out Songs

The magazine *Blender* reports regularly on stars like Snoop Dogg, Eminem, and Ludacris, but the popular music monthly also has a softer side. According to its editors, here are the ten greatest songs to play during a make-out session:

1. "Avalon" by Roxy Music
2. "Turn Off the Lights" by Teddy Pendergrass
3. "Let's Get It On" by Marvin Gaye
4. "Low Down (Nobody Has to Know)" by R. Kelly
5. "If I Was Your Girlfriend" by Prince
6. "November Rain" by Guns N' Roses
7. "Love Serenade" by Barry White
8. "Love to Love You Baby" by Donna Summer
9. "Wild Horses" by The Rolling Stones
10. "All Blues" by Miles Davis

SPINNING THE BOTTLE

The beauty of Spin the Bottle is that it allows kids to kiss without making a commitment. After all, it's a game of chance—where the bottle stops, nobody knows!—so players can't be accused of "liking" anyone.

SPIN THE BOTTLE: NOT JUST FOR KIDS.

The origins of the game are unclear, but many believe it has its roots in cyclomancy—the centuries-old practice of seeing omens in a spinning object, which is usually a wheel (think "wheel of fortune") but sometimes an arrow or a bottle.

What is known is that Spin the Bottle was preceded by a game called Spin the Plate. Popular in both England and the United States, the game called for boys and girls to gather around a plate or pie pan. A boy would spin the plate on its edge, like a top. Before the plate fell flat, he called out the name of a girl he wanted to kiss. If the girl could run forward and grab the plate before it fell, the boy was out of luck; if she couldn't, she had to give the boy a kiss. Next the girl would take a turn, spinning a plate and calling out a boy's name, and so it went.

In their 1936 article "Ozark Mountain Party Games," folklorists Vance Randolph and Nancy Clemens pointed out that Spin the Plate tended to work in favor of boys, who usually wanted a kiss: "The boy usually gives [the girl] very little chance to catch the plate, and kisses her after a terrific struggle—only a brazen hussy would permit the kiss without a struggle." And if the girl was particularly pretty, the boy would feign to stumble and fall on his way to grabbing the plate.

"Any man who can drive safely while kissing a pretty girl is simply not giving the kiss the attention it deserves."

—Albert Einstein

So fervent were ancient Rome's citizens about kissing, they invented three separate words to signify different types of kisses: *oscula* (friendly kisses), *basia* (kisses of love), and *suavia* (passionate kisses).

"What's Your Band Called Then?"

If you're in an Irish pub late at night and they start cranking the Pogues (Irish for "kisses"), try to move away from the crowd. Any open space will likely be invaded by soused young Gaels dancing in that peculiar stomping way that only the Irish seem capable of. Playing an unlikely combination of traditional Irish music and punk, the band's front-man was singer-songwriter Shane McGowan, described by *Rolling Stone* as a "lamprey-mouthed vocalist and legendary boozer." Then why do they have such a nice name? The story goes like this:

McGowan had a spiritual awakening at a Sex Pistols concert in 1975. After seeing Johnny Rotten tear up the stage, he thought, "This is what I want to do with my life!"

In the hard rock and punk scenes, a lot rests on a name. "Everyone was forming bands; it was such a laugh," says McGowan on his Web site. "It was like a competition: What's your band called then?" Thus, he created the Nipple Erectors in 1977. After releasing one single, they broke up. The singer got a job in a record store and joined various bands until 1982, when he formed Pogue Mahone ("Kiss My Ass"). Though the name beautifully communicated the band's roots in both Irish and punk music, it was shortened to the Pogues for "diplomatic" reasons.

Kiss-ful Thinking

Most people will never have the chance to kiss a celebrity, much less the celebrity of their choice. But that doesn't stop fantasizing—or polling. Angelina Jolie came out on top of a 2004 poll of British men's top choices for a celebrity kiss, beating out runners-up Keira Knightley and Halle Berry. Women chose Orlando Bloom over Brad Pitt and George Clooney.

Canadian Content

Meanwhile, Canadians singled out Keanu Reeves and Nelly Furtado as the most kissable of their compatriots.

Pucker Up for the President

And in other poll news, 2004's U.S. presidential candidates faced a thin enough margin in the kissability stakes to rival the election results. With 43 percent of the vote, John Kerry was top choice for kissing, narrowly beating George W. Bush's 41 percent.

"I married the first man I ever kissed. When I tell my children that, they just about throw up."

—Barbara Bush

A Conventional Kiss

Former Vice President Al Gore has been described as dull, boring, stiff, even comatose. The joke section of the Web site www.republicans.org offers this howler: "What's the difference between Al Gore and a slab of Formica? Absolutely nothing."

But anyone who saw the lollapalooza of a kiss Gore laid on his wife Tipper at the 2000 Democratic Convention would have to admit that the candidate was animated, enthused, fired-up, even stoked. Media wonks instantly dubbed Al and Tipper's big moment "The Kiss." Everyone loved it. "The sheer carnality of the kiss—the can't-wait-to-get-back-to-the-hotel-room urgency, the sexual electricity flowing south—was riveting," one *Time* magazine reporter wrote.

And for a short while, Gore rode his lips to the top of the polls. Before the convention, he trailed his opponent, George W. Bush, by about sixteen points; after the convention, the two candidates were neck and neck, thanks to a swell in support from female voters. Of course, speculation ran rampant that the kiss was a planned political move to mark a distinction between Gore and his philandering boss, Bill Clinton.

A politically motivated lip lock from the "inventor of the Internet"? Couldn't be!

Contagious Kisses

If you're allergic to, say, peanuts and you have an allergic reaction immediately after a kiss, the cause should be obvious: While you were getting ready for the date, your partner was munching on a peanut butter sandwich. Mere traces of allergy-causing agents can trigger a reaction.

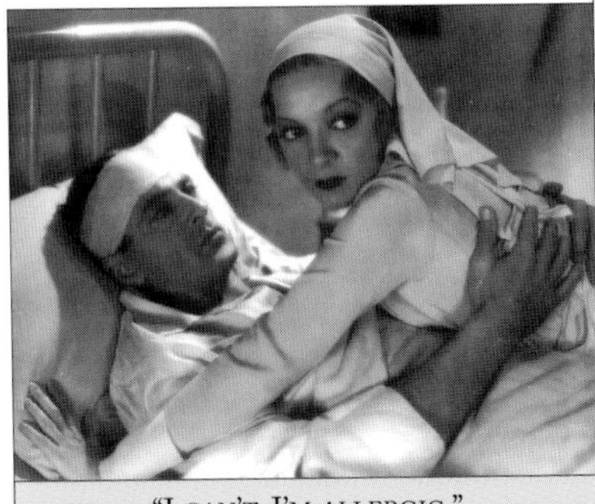

"I CAN'T. I'M ALLERGIC."

If you think you're allergic to nothing and get hives after kissing someone, think again. Your partner might be taking medicine—an antibiotic, for example—to which you're allergic. A case study reported in the medical journal *The Lancet* describes how scientists in Italy learned of this phenomenon when a woman came to the hospital with swollen lips after kissing her husband. The docs couldn't figure out the problem, so they decided to experiment. Over a period of days, they injected the husband with placebos and bacampicillin (the antibiotic he'd taken before the toxic kiss) and had him perform numerous tongue tangos with his wife. They concluded that the husband's antibiotic had, in fact, caused the wife's outbreak.

The frequency of such cases is impossible to determine. When a person arrives in the emergency room with a face full of hives, how many doctors ask about the patient's kissing habits?

"You kiss an actor and you don't know what they are going to smell like. But you kiss a girl and she is going to smell good. And she's very soft. They're soft and they smell nice. Guys don't."

—Actress Julianne Moore on kissing Toni Collette in *The Hours*

BIZARRE KISSING LAW #5: Colorado

They take bedtime seriously here.

A law prohibiting men from kissing women while they're asleep is still on the books in Logan County.

A Nose for Kissing

Kids will kiss "Eskimo-style" by rubbing noses. But if you want to do it right, you'll place your nose against your partner's cheek and *smell* it. This is how the Inuit really kiss, and it's a form of smooching that can be seen in several cultures throughout the world.

It's true that members of some aboriginal tribes have been known to say hello by rubbing noses. Explorer Alfred Russel Wallace refers to this action as the "Malay kiss" in his 1856 log from his travels in the Malay Archipelago. Other tribes will press their nose and mouth to one another's face and draw in a deep breath, smelling and "tasting" their counterpart. As these people take in the other's odor, the theory goes, they believe the souls are intermingling.

The Devil Made Me Do It

"Kiss my ass!" It's a rare and special insult that still packs a punch after hundreds of years. This one dates back to (at least) the fourteenth century. In the Middle Ages, it was commonly believed that Satan himself attended witch initiation ceremonies. At the established moment, he would turn around and the initiate would kiss his posterior as a sign of subservience. This was called the Kiss of Shame or, in Latin, *osculum infame*. Witches have noted that this practice wasn't as debased as it sounds, because the Prince of Darkness actually had a second face where the sun doesn't shine!

The Kiss of Shame.

> "A kiss can be a comma, a question mark, or an exclamation point."
>
> —Mistinguett, French dancer and singer

You're So Sensitive!

Guess what the largest sex organ is. Nope. It's your skin. It's also the most sensitive part of your body. And the periorial area (the lower half of your face) is the most sensitive section of the body. No wonder kisses can pack such a punch.

The lips and tongue are jammed with nerve endings that are wired to the brain. When a person puts his or her orbicularis oris (the muscle used to pucker the lips) to good use and makes contact with another person's lips, the brain releases endorphins and oxytocin hormones. The salivary glands kick into high gear to keep the mouth moist. These potent substances, plus chemicals in the saliva, rocket throughout the body to produce that warm wave of mood enhancement and sexual stimulation that keep us coming back for more. (You can call it love if it makes you happy.)

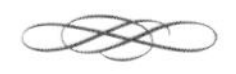

MTV Movie Awards for Best Kiss

1992 – Anna Chlumsky/Macaulay Culkin, *My Girl*

1993 – Rene Russo/Mel Gibson, *Lethal Weapon 3*

1994 – Demi Moore/Woody Harrelson, *Indecent Proposal*

1995 – Lauren Holly/Jim Carrey, *Dumb and Dumber*

1996 – Natasha Henstridge/Matthew Ashford, *Species*

1997 – Vivica A. Fox/Will Smith, *Independence Day*

1998 – Drew Barrymore/Adam Sandler, *The Wedding Singer*

1999 – Gwyneth Paltrow/Joseph Fiennes, *Shakespeare in Love*

2000 – Sarah Michelle Gellar/Selma Blair, *Cruel Intentions*

2001 – Julia Stiles/Sean Patrick Thomas, *Save the Last Dance*

2002 – Jason Biggs/Seann William Scott, *American Pie 2*

2003 – Kirsten Dunst/Tobey Maguire, *Spider-Man*

2004 – Carmen Electra/Amy Smart/Owen Wilson, *Starsky & Hutch*

The Pleasure Principle

If you see yourself doing any kissing in the immediate future, you might want to skip this part. Kissing, according to Freud, can be traced back to your mother's breast—your only source of nourishment before you grew teeth.

Lying around, working the vocal chords, and flailing the limbs just don't cut it for a baby when it comes to the pleasure principle. The warm, fresh milk that results from our sucking—now that's pleasure! When Momma left the room, we learned to jam a thumb into our mouths in a search for more sucking pleasure. Makes sense. The thumb is perfectly convenient: It's always there (unlike Mom) and belongs to no one but you.

Dr. and Mrs. Freud.

The thumb, however, doesn't satisfy us for long. Teeth grow in and we learn to get our nourishment from tearing and chewing. And since you can't have a civilization of people walking around sucking their thumbs, we seek out pleasure in other people's lips: soft, red, and wet—just like mother's nipple.

It's a Feudal Thing

For roughly a thousand years, from the 700s to the 1700s, France existed under a system of feudalism, in which the contract of loyalty between lord and vassal was the foundation of society. The ceremony that made their agreement official was sealed with a kiss.

In short, the lord would offer his vassal a portion of land on which to live and work. In return the vassal provided military service and money or other compensation, along with his undying loyalty. The ceremony putting all of this into play was deadly serious: The vassal shaved his head, kneeled, put his hands between his lord's, and offered an oath of fealty. Then the lord would plant a kiss on the vassal's lips, making the contract official.

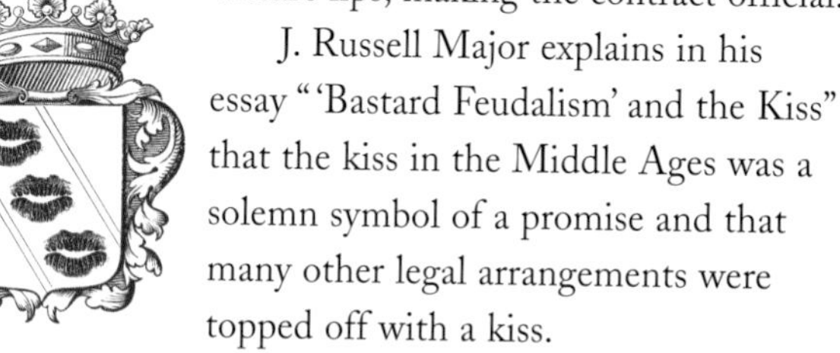

J. Russell Major explains in his essay "'Bastard Feudalism' and the Kiss" that the kiss in the Middle Ages was a solemn symbol of a promise and that many other legal arrangements were topped off with a kiss.

During these ceremonies, it was okay for men to kiss men, but the church frowned upon the idea of churchmen kissing women. Since the church was at the center of the legal system, this was a problem. In the case of a woman finalizing a legal proceeding with a church official, such as acquiring land left to her in a will, a stand-in would often kiss the woman. The fear was great in those days that a kiss would trigger unbridled lust, and churchmen just couldn't take that chance.

This isn't to say that men and women didn't ever kiss romantically. Today a kiss barely means you've reached first base; back then if a man kissed a woman, it was practically a marriage proposal. Put into historical context, it doesn't seem so strange. As Major points out, the concept of marriage was based more on the lord-vassal arrangement than any notions of love and partnership we might have today. The kiss was an extremely important symbol in cementing the relationship between a man and a woman.

"I'll show you some kissing that'll put hair back on your head!"

—George Bailey (Jimmy Stewart)
to a balding townsman,
in *It's a Wonderful Life*

"Hello, May I Smell You?"

Have you ever wondered how the greeting kiss came about? After all, why do we want such a close call with the germs of strangers? In his 1883 book, *Camping Among Cannibals*, the Western explorer Alfred St. Johnston recalls how he was taken aback when he met a tribesman in Fiji: The man grabbed the explorer's hand, drew it up to his nose, and took a great big whiff. The famous Captain Cook visited the Friendly Islands (now Tonga) in the South Pacific, where he saw strangers greet one another by touching noses, then grasping one another's hands and rubbing it on their nose and lips. Explorers theorized that these forms of kissing were not unlike animals smelling one another. If this is the case, that most civilized of kisses—the hand kiss—is surely only one short evolutionary step away from this practice.

Mother's Kiss

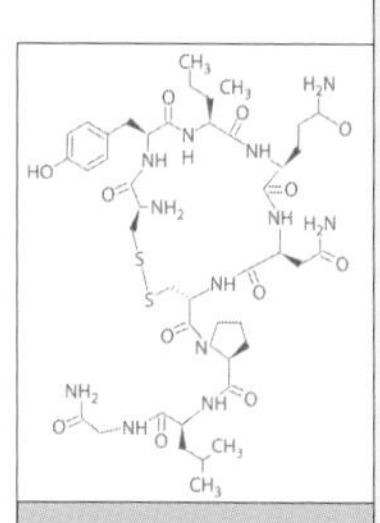

Oxytocin.

We're all born with a "blank slate" of genetics waiting to be activated by our surroundings—and a mother's kiss might be crucial to jump-starting our brains.

If there's one perfect substance in the body, it's oxytocin, a chemical stored in our brain that, when released, makes us feel good all over. A mother's kiss actually functions as an "on" switch for the release of this chemical from the baby's brain. As a result, the child will seek out more contact with the mother in the future (gotta get that rush!) and, therefore, a healthy mother-child bond is developed.

And it's a bond with plenty of long-term health benefits. Research shows that unkissed babies are more likely to end up depressed, stressed out, and lonely later in life. Interestingly enough, another chemical triggered by a kiss is opioid. Just like opium, this hormone moves you closer to literally feeling no pain. Kids with higher levels of opioids coursing through their bodies are likely to handle a scraped knee better than emotionally neglected children. No wonder a kiss from Mom makes every boo-boo better.

The Groom May Now Kiss the Groom

Long before gays and lesbians won (and lost, and won, and lost) the right to marry in places like San Francisco and Boston, there was a time and place where same-sex wedding ceremonies were common—specifically, medieval Europe.

In his book *Same-Sex Unions in Premodern Europe*, medieval historian John Boswell points out that Catholic and Greek Orthodox churches often held same-sex marriage ceremonies between the eighth and sixteenth centuries. The rituals included the couples holding hands, covering one another's face with veils, and tying the knot with a wedding kiss.

This doesn't mean that the union necessarily held the same weight as heterosexual marriage, or that Christian churches condoned same-sex sex. According to Boswell, marriage was largely a business arrangement in those days—with a sprinkle of emotion and a dash of spirituality. Other scholars have compared the ceremony to an authorized bond of friendship and nothing more. Although medieval scholars will continue to argue over what it all means, one thing is clear: The wedding kiss hasn't always been reserved for brides and grooms.

More Kissing Bugs

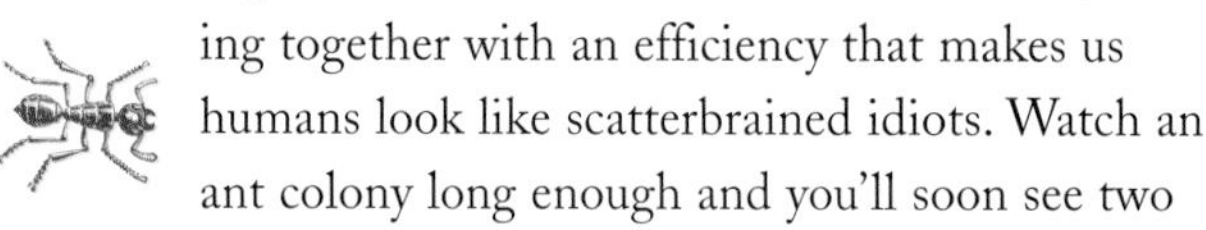

Ants are the great communicators of the insect world, working together with an efficiency that makes us humans look like scatterbrained idiots. Watch an ant colony long enough and you'll soon see two ants "kissing." What they're doing, in fact, is feeding and communicating via a bug version of the French kiss.

Ants eat as they work via a process called *trophallaxis*, in which one ant passes food mouth to mouth to another. Along with the food, the ants also share pheromones—chemical substances that communicate such things as the giver's state of health and task group (hunter or builder). This "trophallactic kiss" is key to the welfare of an ant colony.

Everything comes with a flip side, though. Exterminators take advantage of trophallaxis to spread their poison into the deepest recesses of an ant colony. The result is thousands of tiny kisses of death.

Dogs also engage in trophallaxis. In the wild, puppies inform their parents that it's feeding time by licking their face and, thus, triggering the trophallactic response. When a dog licks you, it's not so much kissing you as asking for a bite to eat.

Kiss (1925) by Pablo Picasso.

Kissers Revolt!

When it comes to making out, the only differences between a car and a canoe are foggy windows. The strict social customs of early twentieth-century America didn't leave much opportunity for the more enjoyable aspects of courtship, so young people had to improvise. In Boston, for instance, they paddled their canoes out into the Charles River for a little private time away from their leering chaperones. Thomas A. McMullin chronicled the subsequent events in his article "Revolt at Riverside."

Canoedling?

In 1903, the puritanical leaders of Boston figured out that all those seemingly empty canoes on the river didn't float out there by themselves; their passengers were lying down—and most likely kissing! "If these canoes could speak, what awful tales they would tell," one minister grumbled. City officials immediately banned kissing in canoes. Problem solved.

Or not. Boston's young boaters didn't appreciate the interference and staged a protest. Countless lovers floated about the river, lying down in their canoes, flagrantly breaking the new rules; when the police approached, they blew kisses at them. Boys too young to kiss in canoes waged guerrilla warfare from the bridges above, shooting beans at the cops patrolling the river. Others conducted psyops on land, placing Victrolas underneath the windows of city officials and blasting offensive songs. Plenty of hot-lipped canoeists were hauled in front of judges and told to pony up twenty dollars in fines.

But over the next few years, arrests started dropping off. And once the automobile became widely available, kissing rebels moved their illicit operations to backseats around Beantown.

"The kiss originated when the first male reptile licked the first female reptile, implying in a subtle, complimentary way that she was as succulent as the small reptile he had for dinner the night before."

—F. Scott Fitzgerald, from his notebooks printed in *The Crack-Up*

Credits

Images on pages
8 (bottom right), 15, 19, 22, 23, 24, 25, 26, 39, 42,
45, 50, 57, 66, 73, 74, 84, 94, 103, 106, 110, 112
courtesy of The Everett Collection, Inc.

Images on pages
13, 28, 31, 35, 54, 61, 72, 82, 86,
88, 90, 96, 100, 118, 125, 126
courtesy of The Granger Collection, New York

Images on pages
16, 40, 58, 64, 71, 77, 119, 123
by Michael Rogalski